My
Confession

**FROM A THOUSAND MEN
TO ONE WOMAN**

Anonymous

Copyright © 2018.

I have tried to recreate events, locales and conversations from my memories of them. In order to maintain their anonymity in some instances I have changed the names of individuals and places, I may have changed some identifying characteristics and details such as physical properties, occupations and places of residence.

My Confession – From a Thousand Men to One Woman/
—1st ed.

Introduction

I have had the same keychain for the last 26 years. It's been pulled in and out of my pockets thousands of times and has dangled from the ignition of lots of vehicles over the years. My grandmother bought it for me... probably just as one of those cute little gifts that you just give someone as a little trinket. It showed up in the mail one day, a little package with a card telling me that she was praying for me.

On the keychain is inscribed a fairly well-known promise found in the Bible's Old Testament.

"For I know the plans I have for you," declares the Lord, *"plans to prosper you and not to harm you, plans to give you hope and a future."*

That verse from the book of Jeremiah is the very thing I read the very first time I ever read the Bible after having my life utterly transformed and turned upside down by Jesus Christ. A promise for a hope and a future. Two things that, just a few months prior, I had just about given up on. Tormented by an abusive father, twisted by the ravages of childhood sexual abuse, and turned away from all sense of normalcy by years of an outlandishly homosexual and promiscuous lifestyle, the last things on my mind were "a hope" and "a future."

Yet, one springtime morning in my kitchen, all of that changed in an instant. All along, the Lord knew the plans that He had for me. And still has for me. Plans to prosper me, and to keep me from harm.

I never asked for it. And I can't even begin to explain how much I don't deserve it. But in an instant, I had a promise of hope, springing from a despair so deep it felt like I was drowning in it.

My grandmother had no idea what had happened in my life when she picked out that keychain and mailed it to me. My fingertips slide over the inscription on that keychain every day.

I've been thinking about writing this book for a long time. Before I got married, I would travel for speaking engagements and lots of people asked me to tell my story. I did that for a few years and then stopped. I didn't like being the evangelical freak show. I felt like I was an exhibit on display, and I didn't like what the Christian culture was casting me as. I was an "ex" something in their marketing. But in reality, I'm not an "ex" anything. Or even a "present" anything. I'm a just a guy. I was a fairly new Christian then. Now I've been a Christian for going on three decades.

About 15 years ago, I completely stopped telling my story. On rare occasions, I'll share bits and pieces of it with a client who is coming to the counseling ministry that I head up. People who come in contact with the ministry might gather that I have some sort of ...background. But they don't know what it is.

I'm a really private person. I really don't have a need to put my story out there for all to read and talk about. However, God has made it clear that it's the time for me to share. I'm sorry that this has to be published anonymously, but for reasons I can't control, this is the only way that I can share my story at this point.

I've tried not to hold a lot back. The first 20 years of my life were very dark, so I want to paint them honestly and bluntly. Because that's the only way the jolt of the contrast can be explained of how everything changed when God showed up.

Honestly telling my story like this feels like I'm turning my skin inside out. But I'm doing it because there are so few testimonies out there about this kind of stuff... of the life-altering process of a person coming from a primary homosexual orientation to a primary heterosexual orientation.

It happened with me because I was given a promise... a promise of hope and of a future. I've clung to that promise every day since my life changed that morning in the kitchen.

I write this to encourage people who are in the same circumstance that I found myself in back then. And I write this to encourage the people who are in a place to help and serve those who desperately need love and grace while they're walking the pathway to healing.

I figure that telling my story in total will help it not to be reduced to a few "juicy" parts. It's the story of God totally interrupting a pagan life that was going down the toilet and then choosing to do an amazing thing with this screwed-up weirdo.

It's the story of God relentlessly pursing me, and blessing me, and shaping me, and healing me. It's the story of how God, in his mercy, completely turned my life around.

It's the story of how God has steadfastly refused to let me become someone less than He intended.

That's the story. It's not the sex I had. It's not the brokenness or the shame. It's God's work to completely transform my life and pull this incredibly messed-up soul along.

So, truthfully, it's not my story at all. It's my confession. But it's God's story.

My "promised future" has, in large part, happened for me. I'll give you all the details on that too. But there's more promise yet to come.

I pray that this story will give you a greater inkling of the promise of God for your own life. For hope and for future.

Chapter I

Everything I remember about my grandparents' house makes me feel loved. I can picture the perfectly manicured front yard. But you bypassed everything in the front if you were family. The front door was just for salesmen and politicians. But the back yard was a wonderland to me as a child. It was completely fenced in with a circle of heirloom roses outside the pathway from the door. There was a huge raspberry bush - and it produced the most delicious berries that my grandmother used to make pies that nearly knocked you down they were so good. Now, I have a line of raspberry bushes just like theirs. Now, my wife and I make jellies.

Probably about a quarter of my grandfather's yard was plowed under for a garden. Plus, there were lots of fruit trees. He grew everything. Absolutely everything. My grandmother, the first generation off the boat from Italy, liked to go scour the garden for something to cook for dinner each night. Oh, and I can't forget the amazing grape arbor. Sometimes we'd set two picnic tables with red checkered tablecloths under that arbor in the summer and enjoy dinner al fresco while the sun went down. He'd always tell us not to climb it and eat the grapes – they needed them for homemade wine. But of course, my cousins and I would sneak a few here and there.

The house itself was a small, white Cape Cod that my grandfather built with his own hands in the 1930's. He was so proud of that house. When he built it, it was in the country, but over the years, the city neighborhoods sort of swallowed it up. That house just smelled like an Italian grandmother's house should smell. It's such a distinct memory for me. My grandmother was the typical first generation Italian-American woman. She loved to serve grandpa, but it wasn't subservience on her part. "It's just how we show love," she'd say. She cooked everything from scratch. Every meal. Every time anyone came to the house, she always fed you. You had to eat. She'd put a bowl of meatballs in front of you... *"mangia mangia*!" There was no arguing. But really, why would you argue?

My mother was the youngest of five children. All of those boisterous Italians on her side were loud and expressive – the total opposite of my father's family. The moment you set foot in my grandparent's house for a family function, it was like you were Norm on the old TV show, *Cheers*. With that first step inside, everyone is calling out your name with a warm welcome.

I can picture everyone gathered around the dining room table hoisting a glass of wine in a toast. There were always platters of food and cookies. And everyone was always hugging. My grandmother and grandfather told me they loved me every single time they saw me. My mother hugged me every day. Though I felt no unconditional love

8

from my father as a child, I certainly felt it from my mother and her family.

My older relatives on my mom's side have told me that I'm a lot like Nin, our nickname for my grandfather. Thankfully, I must have absorbed a few of his qualities in my younger years. The Italian side of my family was (stereotypically) huge. I had dozens of cousins; age-wise, I was pretty much in the middle of the pack. Lots of us lived pretty close together in the Northside neighborhood of Syracuse. Up until I was 15 or so, I still saw my grandparents or at least a group of my cousins at least once a week. That huge family dynamic was a big part of my life. There was always a lot of affection, but that also meant not a lot of connection. If I wanted to, it was pretty easy to get lost in the crowd.

My father is from this stoic, silent military family. My grandfather served with Patton as a quartermaster. With only one exception, all of his five boys went into military service or the reserves. I remember my father and my uncles commenting that my grandfather ran the house like a boot camp. Probably because he didn't know any other way to run it. My growing-up years were happening while the Vietnam War dominated most Americans' lives and conversations. Whenever we were together with my father's family, when they talked, it was about the war. They were all into it, frequently discussing strategy and all of the latest reports from the front.

There's a great picture I have of my father and three of his brothers looking on as my grandfather pins a medal on one of the boys. Everyone in the photo is in uniform, stiff and standing at attention. That picture seems like the quintessential depiction of my father and his childhood.

My father was shaped in that military mold in every way. He was not an emotional person at all. I don't think he told me he loved me until I was, maybe, 13 or so. I don't remember him ever hugging me. He just was not an expressive person at all. He was very Irish Catholic. And, unlike the Italians on my mother's side, his strain of the Irish seemed to work hard to make it appear that nobody likes each other.

But when the chips were down, you would see them all show up when needed. I don't think I ever understood the positives of that type of heritage, because I can really only remember the many instances when that side of the family was unfeeling, indifferent, and unkind. As a child, I really didn't like any of them. The strained relationship I had with my father only made that dislike of the whole group stronger.

For his entire working career, my father only worked for one company - Niagara Mohawk, the power company that served central New York state. He started as a meter reader when he was 18 and worked his way up to be a manager in the control room, controlling the power flow between Syracuse, Rochester, and Albany. I used to love visiting the power plant where he worked from — the control room felt like the bridge of the Starship Enterprise with all of the blinking lights and room-filling computers.

My dad worked for that same power company for his entire life. That's the same company that his father had worked for through his entire life. And the same company that his father had worked for before that. My family didn't move around — they lived in the same neighborhoods and worked the same jobs and thought the same things. My great-grandfather was connected with the local politicians. My great-grandmother would call the mayor directly and complain about a pothole and a truck would be there to fix it within an hour. When it came to small town politicians, they liked to throw their weight around. When people in the neighborhood met my family members, they knew exactly what they were getting. My grandfather and father and me all, literally, had the same name. Which made it pretty hard to feel like there was any chance of breaking out of the mold of generations of sameness. The community and the family all expected a lot from my family over the years. The message was clear for me: I'd best not let them down.But even with all of the expectations, all of those emotional Italians on my mother's side shaped me far more than my father's family and heritage ever did. We had limited contact with my father's extended family while I was growing up, so the influence I received from my mother's side was much stronger. Our house was just a few blocks from my grandparents. Every Sunday we had a big family dinner – and sometimes more gatherings during the week. It was always a party there. That loving, heavily Catholic-focused environment was what really shaped me as a child. Even in my youngest years, I totally absorbed

11

everything about my Catholic faith. I loved every aspect of it. It felt very "whole life encompassing" for me, but not simply because of it being the backdrop for my school, my church, and much of my family. For an artistically oriented person like me, Catholicism can be particularly appealing. Everything about the Catholic faith is very sensuous to me. The art. The colors that change (like when the vestments are green for much of the year, but purple for Lent, red for many of the feasts, etc.) The pungent incense. The touch of the holy water. There's this beautiful, artistic bent to it all. The Catholic faith has always been a very holistic experience for me. It affects my mind, my soul and my senses.As a first-grader in Catholic school, a nun came to talk to my class about her "calling" or vocation. I remember sitting there, wide-eyed, thinking in my seven-year-old mind, "oh, I'm like her." Not that I was going to become a nun, of course, but that calling she spoke of reverberated with me. She was a representative of the church. She clearly had a strong connection with God. I just knew that, somehow, that same type of calling was my future.Though they were both Catholic, my parents' divergent Irish *vs.* Italian backgrounds meant their marriage was considered a "mixed marriage." My father got my mother pregnant while they were dating, so the 1950's culture and the Catholic church basically deemed that they had no choice but to get married. Though in their later years, I asked them both about how they felt then. They had no reason to lie to me when they both said that they loved each other. My father even said he intended to ask her to marry him anyway. So, it wasn't like they were forced together. But they certainly felt pressure from the church to marry and to stay together for the 21 years that they did.

Chapter II

My father was quite an asshole. There's really no other way to describe how he was to me as a child. His biggest issue as a father went far beyond his lack of paternal care; his anger was the core problem. And his constant demands for me to "man up" certainly didn't help matters. He literally destroyed anything I loved that didn't meet his standards of masculinity. Yeah, he was a total and complete asshole for all of my growing up.

I so fondly remember the dinners that I'd have with my mother's family. That was a place and those were times when I knew beyond the shadow of a doubt that people there loved me. But in our own home, my father demanded that we sit and be quiet. In his childhood home, under the orders of his militant father, the six children sat silently as they ate each meal. My father wanted the same thing. That demand is pretty indicative of his nature. He had very little grace then. He was frustrated in his marriage, frustrated with his son, and just generally unhappy with life.

His anger fueled everything. Sure, he was not particularly empathetic and rarely thought about other people. But his anger exacerbated all the rest. He hit me all the time. Even when I was as young as 3 or 4, I remember him slapping me on the side of the head, or grabbing me by the shoulders and shaking me. My childhood is filled with those memories of him.

My father's hands were huge. That's what I'd focus on when he hit me — seeing those huge hands coming toward me. He never hit me with a belt or anything like that, but he regularly employed his trademark move: backing me up against the wall. He'd slap me as he taunted me. I was always trapped against the damn wall when he would loom over me, spitting in my face and poking his thick finger into my chest. He'd lose it regularly on me. At least once a week from some of my earliest years through my mid-teens, he'd get mad and just beat the hell out of me.

I wasn't always the one who made him angry, but for some reason when he got mad, he'd consistently focus his rage on me. Of course, I was always thought it was my fault. That I was a bad kid and a huge failure and disappointment. I never was what my father wanted me to be and I was never doing what he wanted me to do. I was always wrong. I would lie awake at night wondering why he didn't love me.

My mother was my protector — sometimes she'd try to intervene, but she could do little to stop him. He never beat me when the rest of the family was around. He sent me to the emergency room once. I was probably 12 or 13. We got into a screaming match in the kitchen. When he

15

went to hit me on the side of the head, he missed a little bit and his fingernails scratched over both of my eyes. I screamed and clutched my face. He took me to the emergency room because it quickly became apparent that I couldn't see out of one eye. His fingernails had scratched both of my corneas. The doctor and nurse asked me how it happened. I didn't hesitate: "my father hit me." I told them exactly what he'd done. I desperately hoped they would call the police, but nothing happened. No police came. No one asked anything else. Nothing. It was the late 1970's and things were different then. I guess my father talked to the doctors after they treated me and smoothed things over.

On a few other occasions, I remember reaching out to a few people in authority to plead for help. But no one ever got involved. Within my extended family, it pretty much went unnoticed. There were plenty of times that I had marks and bruises, but I think my relatives just assumed they were a natural occurrence from roughhousing and playing. Plus, in those days, there was definitely more shame in talking about those types of topics openly. It might have been something that the women might whisper about quietly in the kitchen, but it would have been highly unlikely for someone to directly address the issue. Plus, my grandfather had just emigrated from Italy a few decades before...culturally, he would have NEVER had those kinds of conversations. But my father is certainly lucky that he never knew. It wouldn't have been pretty.

Still, I wonder what would have happened if I was able to overcome my fear and shame and reach out to my extended family.

Finally, I got tall enough and strong enough to change things. My father had me backed against a wall and was yelling at me, berating me while he poked his finger in my chest. And as a 16-year-old with just enough courage, I punched him in the side of the head.

He was taken aback, looking at me completely shocked. Then he punched me back. We had a knock-down fight for probably a good ten minutes. I slammed his head into the wall and broke the thermostat. He cut himself on the broken glass and I felt a real sense of accomplishment to see blood running down the side of his face. He pulled back, heaving and out of breath. "You had enough?" he growled...obviously trying to end the altercation. I didn't answer and went after him again, landing some more punches.

That was the day when things changed, because my father never hit me again. That was a huge moment for me - I was finally enough of a man to break off his physical assaults. But boy, prior to that point, I took it from him through my entire childhood.

Every time he beat me, the fire of hatred I had toward him flamed up even higher. My father was just this big scary bully. Along with hitting me, he was really verbally abusive. If he thought that I screwed up, I got screamed at. "You dumb son of a bitch!" He constantly told me I was stupid and dumb. He never said he was proud of me. Nothing positive, ever.

17

Up through my mid-teens, my father's actions couldn't have been in more stark contrast to how my mother treated me. She'd always smile as she showered me with compliments. "You're smart! You're funny!" Really, she was just calling out my identity in ways that my father should have, but was simply unable to do.

I have this old black and white photo of my first communion – it's such a stark depiction of my relationship with each of my parents. My mother and I are clutching each other, while my father touches no one as he stands at attention in his ramrod military posture. Though we're in church, it's almost like he thinks he's in military formation or something. That photo is pretty much my childhood in a nutshell. My father looming and rigid and off to the side, while my mother and I try lean into each other for comfort from this asshole.

I had always strongly identified with my mother and her significantly more emotive side of the family. And felt deeply polarized from my father and his side of the family. That early and obvious distance from him marked me in my mind... and in his....as a failure. That I was a break in the line that stretched back for generations. That my mere existence caused a disconnect with all that was a male in my family. This has always created a deep internal drama in me. And a deep, deep shame that made me feel like I was supposed to be someone very different than who I was.

Over time, that disconnect also turned into a masculine/feminine thing in my mind. That I was actually shaped in the mold of my mother, not my father. I was just soft. I was a nature lover. I loved taking care of animals. I liked growing plants and helping my mother's father tend to his beautiful rose garden and grape arbor.

But my understanding of men from my father and his long line of military ancestors was that real men are blood and guts. Real men swear and smoke. Real men are tough and they most assuredly did not cry.

I cried all the time. Still do quite a bit, actually.

I was given a clear and concrete definition of the man that I was expected to grow up to be. But I had no way to get there. I knew from the start that no part of me would fit in that militant mold. I was this other thing. Soft, passionate, emotive. I was from a long line of warriors, but I was a nurturer. The chasm between who I was and who my father demanded that I become was great. And I had no idea how to bridge the divide.

This deep fracture marked my identity from as early as I can remember. I was a male growing up in a household with a hyper-masculine father. But I was coddled and protected by a mother who didn't want to see my soft, artistic tendencies crushed. I really was fundamentally a broken kid. There was almost two of me competing within. But the masculine side of me started becoming more and more invisible because, ultimately, I was determined not to be anything like my father. I hated him. I loved my mother and her family. I hated my father and his family, and I couldn't stand the thought that anything about me resemble him at all.

Chapter III

Every human being needs a Father's love. We all have that need programmed into our DNA. You need a father's particular style of nurturing and affection. And if you don't get it, you're going to go looking for it somewhere else. As a child, I sought it out from my friends. Through my elementary and middle school years, my male friends were extremely important to me, I think, because I was unconsciously trying to fill the male deficit in my life.

I was part of a group of boys, mostly Italians like me, who ran together in school and in the neighborhood. We all did just about everything together, right up until my family moved out to the suburbs when I was in the fourth grade.

These neighborhood boys and the church were the most significant anchors in my life as a child. I was a wide-eyed Catholic boy who loved all things about the church. The heritage. The mysticism. The power that it held in my family. I went to mass at the same church that my grandparents had gone to for most of their time in

America. My cousins all went to the same church too – and the same Catholic school.

All this was happening only about a decade after Vatican II, so the church still had this really mystical, old-world European kind of feel. My extended family was always all in for all of the festivals and the holy days. I just really loved everything about it. It was the grand, common element that tied everything together for my family and even the neighborhood boys I loved being with. Honestly, I look back at that time as being one of the best periods I can remember. Yeah, the drama with my father was certainly there, but there were also a lot of good things that shaped me during that time... most of which I didn't clearly see until I was older.

I was 10 when we left that neighborhood that I loved and moved to the suburbs. Gone was the ethnic, gritty, super-Catholic neighborhood that I roamed with my friends and cousins. The new normal was a middle-class white, boring subdivision full of people trying to move up in the world.

My parents were determined to be upwardly mobile. I think every immigrant family, especially those who are first- or second-generation Americans, feels the pressure to be scaling the ladder of financial success. It's the understood goal for immigrants that you need to beat your parents in financial wherewithal. In other words, if you've made the jump to live in America, it's important that you make more money and have more stuff than the generations before you. I think that pressure drove my father a little bit nuts to have to put on those types of airs since he was pretty conservative financially. My mother, on the other hand, was a spender. She really valued how money could help her to have fun and appear well off to her friends. Her constant willingness to loosen the purse strings led to a unending source of fuel for arguments with my father over money. This whole idea of financial well-being, founded or not, is what drove my family's move to the suburbs.

Living in the suburbs was a completely different culture. A different everything that I never really grew accustomed to. It suited my mother to get away from the ethnic environment where she'd spent her whole life. The rest of my nuclear family also adapted pretty well to the move. I was the only one who felt incredibly out of place. There were no boys around for me to hang out with, so I lost that strong male connection. And I got bullied a lot because I was the smart kid in class who had no friends. That bullying only set off more alarms in my head that I was abnormal... that there was always something wrong with me.

For various reasons, I seemed to never really get into a good situation with enduring male friendships like I'd had before. Either they got cut off due to extenuating circumstances, or I screwed things up. There was one nerdy kid in seventh grade with me who was consistently picked on by all of the other kids. I didn't mind him though. We hung out and slept over at each other's houses sometimes. But one day when he wasn't around at school, some of the other guys in the class were ripping on me for being friends with him. Even though we'd been doing things together for like a year, I yelled back "I'm not friends with him. I think he's weird!"

I turned around, then, to see the kid standing in the doorway of the classroom. He burst into tears and walked off. As you might guess, we were never friends again after that. I tried to talk to him and apologize, but he would just push me away. After that he transferred schools. I can still see him in my mind. I should try to find him and apologize. But that whole mishap was just another relational failure for me.

Through middle school, it was hard for me to choose anything besides isolating and insulating myself. My home life with my father was awful and I sucked at making and keeping friends. I pretty much turned inward and stayed there. What few friends I had were mostly girls.

Plus, everyone I went to school with, it seemed, was getting into sports. My father would spend every weekend sitting in his chair watching sports on TV. Athletics in general held zero appeal for me. I wasn't good at playing them and I thought watching them was ridiculously boring. Now if you needed someone to draw a still life of a fruit bowl, I was your guy. But being in such a sports-oriented school, my shortcomings in that realm were super apparent. That was just another reason, besides my nerdy existence, that I got picked on terribly. I'd lost all the friends who I loved in my old neighborhood and felt like I had nothing but a whole pile of reasons to "don't even bother trying" when it came to trying to find new relationships. At home, my parents were starting to fight all the time. I really didn't have any place to go.

Chapter IV

I have one older sister. She's four years my senior, and growing up, she was much more in the mold that my father wanted for his children than me. She was far less emotive than me, and much more athletic as she was the star of her high school basketball team. Eventually, my sister ended up as the first female regimental commander of a military academy. She was absolutely the favored one in my father's eyes.

She was maybe 16 or so when she started dating a guy who was a couple years her senior. It was pretty obvious that my parents were not thrilled with this relationship. In retrospect, he was so wrong for my disciplined and goal-oriented sister. I have no idea why she was dating him. He was a gamer, simply consumed by role-playing games like Dungeons and Dragons. He was all about going to renaissance faires. He ended up dating her off and on for a couple of years, but nothing ever turned terribly serious between them.

I really liked this guy. He was fun and emotive. And, selfishly, he paid attention to me. There were so few males in my life at that point, young or old, that didn't ridicule me. I was amazed at how comfortable I felt around him. It didn't take much time for him to become a significant figure in my life.

It was a hot summer in between my 8th- and 9th-grade years. It wasn't long after we had moved to the suburbs, so I was dealing with that change. And I was just hitting the beginning stages of puberty and sprouted a few new hairs on various parts of my body. I started to look a little old for my age. That was the summer when the boundary between my sister's boyfriend and me crumbled and my relationship with him went from emotional to sexual.

He was 21. I was 12.

It was bad. It was damaging. It was wrong. It was a lot of things.

But a part of me liked it.

I could sense the deep schism inside me as I responded in two different ways.

The part of me shaped by my religious upbringing and softened by my tender nature understood that this was horrendous.

But there was another part of me that was self-loathing at my inability to have normal relationships, that was torn up by my parents' long-expected split that summer, and that was becoming a man physically (but was completely clueless emotionally). That was the part that liked it.

This 21-year-old man had already spent years being kind to me and was one of the few positive attachments in my life. I embraced the sexual advances and the sexual part of our relationship because there was, truthfully, a lot that I enjoyed about it.

I enjoyed being held by him. I enjoyed the intimacy. The time alone with his undivided attention. The lying together and talking. The empowering feeling that I was capable of captivating and holding an adult male's attention. The connection I had with him was so potent, so .... soothing, that I began to not care about the other part.

This wasn't just a one-time circumstance of a pervert molesting a kid in an alley. I had a definite connection to him... so much so that, at times, I would initiate our trysts. I would call him to ask to get together. We had a set rendezvous spot a couple blocks away from my home. He would pick me up there and then we'd spend the day together. It certainly wasn't like I was an unwilling victim in this.

This all went on for about a year and a half. But I took care to hide everything about it from my family. They never knew anything about it until years later.

———————————————

I was a 12-year-old boy when this started. But my life experience up to that point was pretty different than the average pre-teen boy. Because of the neglect I had known in my household, I had learned to be very self-sufficient. So I think I felt older than what I was. In my immature 12-year-old mind, it felt like I was having a relationship with this man as an equal.

I'm in my early 50's as I'm writing this and it's easy to look back at a relationship of a 12-year-old with a 21-year-old and see the horror and abuse and the criminality of what was going on. But my experience at the time sure felt like a positive. I was already so messed up and damaged. It felt good to me, and I just didn't give a shit anymore about what anyone else thought.

That relationship, warped as it was, solved a lot of problems for me. He gave me time and attention. He slipped me money when I needed it. He told me he loved me. He held me close after whatever sex act we'd just finished. He affirmed me. "You're a good looking kid, you know that? You're smart. You can figure this out. You can do this." Everything he was saying... everything he was doing... it was all making me feel good. And the intimacy of it all whispered into the gaping voids that riddled and wracked my self-esteem.

By this point, nothing else in my life had any real value to me. Not the church or anything spiritual. Not my family or friends. Once this relationship started, nothing much mattered beyond this makes me feel good. I want to do this again. Plus by this point he was giving me money and gifts. He was paying attention to me. Horrendous morphed into "who cares".

But even with all of the responses that my misshapen 12-year-old psyche translated as positive, I knew the damage was done.

Chapter V

Three months after the abuse started, my parents finally separated. My mother and I moved to our own apartment, and my sister left for college. My mother was working a lot just to make ends meet. She didn't, and honestly couldn't, pay very much attention to me. But there wasn't much she could do to control me anyway by that point. Physically, I was becoming a young man. I was taller than her and she certainly couldn't push me around. But that didn't really matter. She never knew what I was doing, where I was going, or who I was spending my time with.

I started skipping school like crazy. I just didn't want to go. I started to feel like I was an adult and the whole system wasn't working for me.

In this season of my artificial maturity, I also lost my faith. Until that summer when the abuse started, I still believed. I believed in God. I believed in the goodness of the Church. I believed in family.

But everything started to change all at once. The abuse that was already altering my life began just as I was starting puberty. And I watched my parents' marriage dissolve. All the things that the church had taught me just starting feeling like a huge lie. That's what I thought. "This is a lie. It's all a lie. Everything the church says is a lie. Marriage is a lie. Happy families don't exist. It's just all bullshit." My suburban life with a family that supposedly professed faith... it was a prison. It was a huge lie. And now it was shattered.

Outside of the scope of my messed up life, lots of significant cultural changes were going on too. It was the national malaise of the late 70's with long gas lines and hostages in Iran. The sexual revolution had taken a firm hold and the shifting attitude toward all of that was starting to really affect the fabric of American culture. The nation felt like it was gripped by change.

Even as a young teen, I very much embraced the zeitgeist. And my mother fueled some of that because she was feeling especially liberated after escaping from the ties my father had imposed on her. Because of my father, I viewed all men as being abusive and awful. I was determined not to be like that when I grow up. And my mother affirmed that in me. "Yeah, don't be like him. Don't be like him. Men are pigs. Men are awful."

She was so negative about all things dealing with men that it only reinforced my question: Why would I want to be one of the monsters?

My parents were tired. Their marriage was over. And they were both focused on their own lives. My sister was gone to college. I was still going to high school, but I was really just lost in the shuffle. In the evenings, I was either alone or with the guy who was abusing me.

At this point, it felt like I had little more to lose. But I was wrong.

While I was living with my mother in an apartment, she started dating. A lot. And it became the norm for some of her boyfriends to spend the night. She wasn't demure about enjoying this new found freedom she was experiencing. Actually, I felt exposed to my mother's sexuality in a rather shocking, unhealthy, and distressing way. I just couldn't deal with this new and uninhibited behavior from her. It was also, weirdly, making me more aware of my own sexuality. There was some weird, icky emotional stuff this was bringing about in me. Now, my mother never did anything un-right toward me, but something inside of me definitely got more twisted during that period. I was aware of things I shouldn't have been aware of, and seeing and hearing things that no kid should have to experience at that age.

My parents were separated, but hadn't yet divorced. So, periodically, my dad and I would see each other and he'd ask me what my mother was up to. I never knew what to say. I think he wanted me to serve as a go-between for the two of them. And to tell him all the dirt about what my mother was up to. I was soon starting high school. Seriously, what 14-year-old boy wants to be caught in the middle of all that?

I was just getting more and more angry. I couldn't process what was going on and I had no idea how to handle my feelings. My mother couldn't handle me. Honestly, I think part of my anger was a reaction to her being kind of slutty. Ironically, my anger ended up reminding her of my father. Plus, my physicality was changing as I matured. My voice was getting deeper. I think I was starting to remind her of my dad because I'd angrily push her away and snap at her.

She wanted to live her single life. She couldn't be a mother anymore... she basically admitted that to me. "I can't mother you anymore. I need to live my own life and go do my own thing." So after about nine months of living with her and her boyfriends, it happened. She told me she wanted me to go back to living with my father.

I was devastated. I felt so incredibly betrayed by her. She was kicking me out to go live with my monster of an abusive father. Up to that point, I had spent my entire childhood on the same "side" with her. We'd spent much of my life aligned against my father. She was the person who saved me from my father's wrath. She'd put herself figuratively and bodily between my father and me, screaming at him to stop. So my mother was very much my "savior" and my person. She was the only one who I had ever really been open-hearted with. Until now.

I was out of my mind betrayed by her. I screamed "you're a fucking WHORE!" at her. I held nothing back. I couldn't deal with the thought of having to live with my father again. She knew full well how horrible the thought was to me. The betrayal was just so strong. This poured gasoline on all of this negativity that I had and promoted a deep distrust of women for me.

I started to emotionally shut down toward everything and everyone. Everything dealing with family was a lie. I had never felt so absolutely alone. Well, alone except for one connection: the guy who was molesting me.

Chapter VI

So, it happened. I was back to living with my father after my mother kicked me out. He was working double shifts at the power plant to try and keep paying the mortgage on the house where we'd all lived before the separation. I was at school during the day and he went to work around 4 p.m. and worked through much of the night. So in some ways, it was a lot like it had been living with my mother...I rarely saw him. My father certainly wasn't an engaged type of person, so even when he was around we didn't really interact anyhow. I had a bedroom in that house and that was about it.

With such a big family void in my life now, my whole world became centered around one person: my abuser. I was emotionally dependent on him. I was socially dependent on him. And I became financially dependent on him, but he never had enough money to really support me full time.

So, it slowly started dawning on me. What I needed was more of him. Not more of him as an individual, but more of what he was giving me. More money. More emotional support. And more intimacy in the form of sex.

I was about 14 but probably looked more like I was 17. Figuring that that was an advantage for me, I played up this false portrayal of maturity and started sneaking into gay bars. I didn't seem to have a problem getting guys to buy me drinks, so my weekends started to be defined by drinking and enjoying the attention of older men. And it soon became clear that it would be easy to start finding more.

———————————————

I went to a Catholic high school on the opposite end of town from where my dad lived. If I took the school bus, it was about an hour and a half ride. To avoid that, I often took a city bus to get home quicker. I'd often see a guy in his late 30's who was riding the bus home from his job. He had curly hair and was a little paunchy. It wasn't unusual for me to catch him staring at me while we rode the bus. He'd smile at me and I'd look away. Then, one afternoon he got up and moved to the seat across the aisle from me and started up a conversation. I could just tell he was gay. And he was picking up those vibes from me...the 14-year-old kid who he'd been watching for weeks.

I wasn't asking for it. I wasn't flirting. But somehow he sensed that I was an easy target. His approach was crass, but I was intrigued. He asked me to go home with him. I looked at him and considered my options.

"I'll do it, but you have to pay me 50 bucks."

He didn't hesitate. We got off the bus a few stops later, walked to his dated apartment, and he paid me $50 for sex.

There was nothing about Harry that I found to be physically attractive. It was completely about the money for me. I never would have slept with him if he had balked about the price.

Harry was not my first sexual encounter after the abuser. But he became my first regular customer. It was pretty easy actually. I could get off the bus at his stop, do what he asked me to sexually, collect my money, and then walk back to my dad's house from there. I could get away with it without anyone realizing what was going on. It was a total secret.

By the time I started with Harry, I had slept with several men. Most of them were men I had met at the bars. Some were just a little older than me. Some were considerably older....like in their 50's and 60's. Those were the ones who would reciprocate with gifts.

The idea of getting money for sex was very powerful for me. My parents were too busy screwing up their own individual lives to give me much financial support. Plus, I was completely consumed with the idea that I could get enough money to not have to keep living with my father.

It became clear that I needed to increase my "inventory." I needed to find more older men who had money and were willing to pay. So I increased my availability and said 'yes' to pretty much any older guy who had the cash. A few tawdry sex acts for each of these messed up men honestly seemed like a pretty good bargain for the financial independence that I was quickly starting to gain. (Oh my, to be writing this at 51 and looking back at this....) I was too young to get a legal job, but I could do this. I could sell my body for an older man's perverted pleasure.

By this point, the "horrendous" aspect of sex with older men had pretty much disappeared in me. My emotional drive to be with with men was growing stronger each day. I liked being with them. I wanted to sleep with them. I enjoyed the closeness and connection with men who were older. That pattern was already well established in me. I called them my "boyfriends"... like we were having some sort of a romance. And the fact that I got money from them was actually secondary to the feeling that I got from it. The stilling of my inner scream. That was my primary engine of compulsion.

My life became a double life. I was going to a Catholic high school during the day, dutifully putting on my uniform and doing my class work. I went to pep rallies and football games and had at least a smattering of the traditional high school experience. Then I would go home, spray dye my hair, pop my earring in and hit the gay bars to troll for older men with pocketfuls of cash who needed to get their jollies from sex with a high school boy. I did that for my entire sophomore and junior years of high school. It was completely a double life. But I was totally used to being two things after all of my growing up years. I was great at keeping the two segments separate, for it wasn't until I got another job that anyone really realized what I was doing. Just a couple of my friends knew what was going on. Conversely, I never talked about my life as a high school student with my "boyfriends." I wanted them to see me in a different way.

I needed money, so I'd take it when the situation led to that. But I sometimes slept with men with no money exchanged during that period also. They'd proposition me and I'd tell them that they had to pay me. I was bad at it. I was a bad prostitute. I didn't do well with the sales aspect of it. So sometimes they wouldn't pay me and I'd still do what they asked. When they did go ahead and pay, I thought of it as gifts...just gentlemen giving me gifts in exchange for quick sex acts. It was easier to lie to myself because I didn't want to identify myself as a whore. Ironically, I was embracing a similar lifestyle as my mom. But I was still so angry with her then, I would never admit such a thing.

I could look around and see others in my same situation and plenty of boys my age who were doing even more than me. And then I started seeing where they ended up. Drug use was very prevalent in the "call boy" scene. I tried every drug, just like I tried every sex act. Actually, the only thing I didn't do was shoot up. It was meth back then. It was offered to me, but I saw how quickly those boys decompensated who did that. Mushrooms, pot, cocaine...none of that bothered me. But shooting up meth was past my limit. At least I could feel like I had some standard that I wasn't going to totally throw everything away.

The scarier proposition was due to the high murder rate in Syracuse at the time. Call boys were literally disappearing. Some of the guys I'd seen working the bars ended up dead. I didn't need the money that badly. So my time spent in truly casual prostitution was only about 2 years. Then I got a job when I was 17. I was finally old enough to get a normal job and earn some money in a more respectable fashion. And I moved out of my father's house at the end of my junior year in high school. I got out of there as quickly as I practically could. But even during those two years when I was living in his house, I had no connection, emotional or otherwise, with my father.

Through that whole time, I would dream that all of this was leading toward a season of bliss for me. My fantasy was well-formed: I was going to get away from my parents, meet a man and fall in love, and be whisked away from this wretched life. This was the era of *Pretty Woman* when things like that happening actually seemed possible to someone like me.

Once I started being with more men, my relationship with the abuser began to fade away. And when the two of us started spending less time together, he started feeling somewhat guilty. I don't know if he was even aware of the other men. My "need" to be with him diminished as I was with more and more men. I had discovered a new supply line. He started a relationship with a woman and I think he wanted to pursue some sort of normalcy in his life. We had a strained conversation. "We really shouldn't be doing this," he said. "I want to get married some day. And have a kid." That statement from him has HAUNTED ME. As an adult, unless there has been some sort of major intervention and healing in his life, this man still has his abusive tendencies. Statistically, there's a very high

40

likelihood that he's done it again... perhaps even to his own children. And by me not reporting what he did to me... well, it's still something that I struggle with.

That same line of thinking and regret comes up all the time with rape victims that we serve at the counseling ministry that I head up. The victim coming for help realizes that the perpetrator has done it to three other women. And she never called the cops. But you just can't put that kind of pressure on yourself. When you're dealing with the kind of pain that the perpetrator caused, you may not ever have the capacity to make that kind of call. We have to help these victims overcome their guilt that they "let" the abuser or the rapist do it to someone else. They didn't cause the violation. They aren't responsible.

But in my case, I do wish I would have told somebody about him. But I figured that if nobody in the E.R. believed me when I told them my father had scratched my eyeballs, there seemed little hope anyone would have believed me about my abuser.

Chapter VII

I was 15 when I told my father I was gay. It was the first time I ever saw him cry. I had been out turning tricks with a guy and my father picked me up soon afterward. When I got in the car, his face sort of contorted. "I can smell sex on you." Oh my, I was so embarrassed. Decades later, I am still mortified that he said that to me.

He asked me if I was gay.

"Yes. I was having sex with that man," I said, pointing out the car window at a guy walking on the sidewalk. He said nothing and we drove home. We went out on the back deck and he cried. It totally broke him.

By then I was past my embarrassment. I watched him cry... and I loved it.

"It's my fault," he said softly.

"No, it's not your fault," I responded. "People are just born this way. It has nothing to do with you."

It's interesting that I lied to him. But he felt like it was his fault. This was the year after my mother left and he was free falling into his dark, broken period. He was just starting to change before I left for Oregon. I'm sure I contributed to his breaking.

I don't really remember coming out to my mother. Just a conversation when my older sister made a smart ass remark. We were all sitting in the living room and my mother remarked out the blue to me, "You're so handsome. Look at those beautiful eyelashes and those beautiful green eyes."

"You could probably get any girl you want," she continued.

And my sister snorted back, "He can get all the boys that he wants too." My mother said nothing, but I could tell that that's the first time it dawned on her that I was gay. I don't think we ever directly had that conversation. Life just went on without the discussion.

While I was sleeping with older men for money, I was trying to maintain some semblance of being a typical teenager when I was nearing the end of my time in a Catholic high school. My uncle was one of the principals of my school so there was someone who was connected with my family who had their eye on me every day. So, I felt like I had to try and maintain a shell of normalcy.

Even as a 17-year-old with a fairly warped sense of what was normal in life, I knew that a life of exchanging sex for money was not going to land me the all-consuming type of relationship that I craved. The fairy tale depicted in the movie *Pretty Woman* is a pretty unlikely scenario for anyone who is turning tricks, whether gay or straight. So I

43

got two part-time jobs to earn some cash to pay the bills since I was still living on my own.

I got my own apartment and started working at a drug store downtown and in the gift shop of an art museum. I loved that museum job. It allowed me to meet all sorts of gay, creative men. I had a torrid affair with a dancer from the Hartford ballet that went on for like 2 years. But he honestly was just a blip on the radar of all of the encounters I was having at that point. I would go to high school by day, work in the evenings and weekends, and go out almost nightly until 2 a.m., then sleep a few hours and start all over again the next day.

I was just compulsive. There's really no other word for it. It was pretty typical for me to sleep with four or five guys over the course of a week. I was insatiable in this quest for intimacy...for attention. You'd think I would have realized after a handful of attempts that that approach wasn't going to work in finding love, or at the very least, someone to actually care about me. But I just kept trying.

The next one will be the one.

No — the next one will be the one. Honestly, it's amazing I was able to keep that up for so long.

Eventually I moved in with Dominic, an Italian man four years older than me. He was a musician and a computer guy. I thought for awhile that I might have a long-term chance with him, but we ended up only being together a few months. And I certainly wasn't monogamous when we were.

Actually, it's almost funny... we split up because I had sex with a young woman I worked with at the drug store. She was an assistant manager and I wanted a promotion - it was a purely manipulative move on my part. But Dominic just couldn't handle sharing me with a woman. In the course of a month's time, I was probably with several dozen other men, but having sex with a woman was what ended the relationship with Dominic.

I did have a few fleeting moments of interest in women beyond just being their fabulous gay friend. There was one girl who I liked through much of high school, and a few others who I kissed. Then I slept with this woman in hopes of getting a promotion at my job. I guess I was doing a little experimenting with the thought of heterosexuality.

But there was a significant deterrent with that experimentation for me: my father had gotten my mother pregnant as a teenager. I was so incredibly determined to be nothing at all like him that I truly feared getting some girl pregnant... and thereby starting to repeat my father's life. Any minor interest I had in straight sex paled due to the pregnancy concern. That fear also reinforced in my mind that gay sex was just easier. It was always available for me. I could even get money for it when I needed to pay the bills. Plus, there was a significant emotional component in it for me...in that big aching part of my soul that was filled with father and peer rejection. Sex with another male, be it an older man or a peer, would temporarily assuage that big hurt in the center of my heart.

So, back to Dominic. Actually, splitting up with him only meant that I moved into another bedroom in the

45

apartment and we split the rent. We got a third roommate, Melissa, to rent the last bedroom. Melissa was wild. She had that iconic Cyndi Lauper lopsided 80's hair and partied a lot. My friends and I used to do drugs with her and her musician boyfriend, Curt, a total Bon Jovi look-a-like, hair band guy. Pot, coke, mushrooms...they were all frequent guests in our apartment. Hey, sex and drugs and the 80's, man.

I was starting to really spiral out of control. Nearly every night now, I was hitting the bars and would go home with a different random guy. I was infatuated with this prostitute named Vincent Bianchi. He was a hairdresser by day, and a hooker by night. I desperately wanted to date him and thought he was incredibly good looking. We hooked up a few times, but he had no real interest in a relationship with me. What he was interest in, however, was using me as a good upsell for his services. He was always wanting me to go on tricks with him, because men would pay more to watch him and I do it together. Plus, he was probably 21 and I was only 17 ... so there was that added kink for the johns. I felt like I loved him and was euphoric the times that I got to have sex with him. I was so messed up. This period of my life with all of its twisted stories could be a bad movie.

Through that time period, I felt more compelled to wrap myself in the gay persona. The AIDS crisis of the 1980's was starting. I would play the role and go to

ACTUP meetings and I did a thing with the AIDS quilt in Syracuse. Truly, I was starting to really embrace the identity of being gay.

This all went on for about a year and a half. Then I moved out from the apartment, and went back to staying at my father's house just for a summer while I started plotting how I could move away from Syracuse. He had gotten remarried by this point. I also ended up finishing high school early. I'd spent three years in a catholic high that taught at higher standards than the public schools at the time. I transferred to a public school just so I could graduate early. I was wicked smart and driven. I was just living in two completely different worlds.

I felt so adult with all of my encounters and I wanted to start living an adult life on every level. But to do this I knew I'd have to get out of town. I was always surrounded by constant reminders of my childhood and my family. If I wanted to really become something other than what Syracuse represented to me, I knew I'd have to move far away   to   do   it.

Chapter VIII

I n the 1980's (long before the days of the internet), there was an advertised network where a male in his late teens could become a hot commodity by putting himself up for bidding. Men from all over the country were looking for boys in their teens to live with them and serve as a house boy or a companion. A large, national gay magazine would feature classified ads where these house boys would be solicited.

"Sugar Daddy actively seeking fit, firm teen as live-in companion."

Or, if you wanted to put yourself out there for hire - like I did at the time - you could put an ad in the magazine describing a particular setup and watch the eager responses roll in to your mailbox. Honestly, within a couple of weeks of when I placed the classified ad, I had hundreds of responses. I didn't know fully what I was looking for yet, but I thought I'd find one that seemed like a better situation than being out whoring all night.

I opened up all of the envelopes, and looked at the photographs of these men, and read how they described their living situation and what they wanted to offer me. I followed up with maybe a dozen of them and sent a picture of myself. Then I narrowed it down to just four and set up times to go visit with each of them. They all lived in different cities and I asked them each to pay for all of my expenses to come. I told them each I would stay a week. I figured that would be enough time to see if I liked the guy, and if I liked his house. And I gave some thought about what part of the country I might like to live in. The third visit I made was to a best-selling author of Norwegian descent who lived in Portland, Oregon. And after my week-long "trial" with him, I stayed.

This guy's first book had put him on the radar of lots of promoters, and got him interviews on all of the big TV talk shows. He had lots of rich, gay friends, and lived in a fabulous mansion near Portland and had an equally fabulous apartment in the city. When I moved into his house, he could have been an axe murderer for all I knew. He'd told me that he just wanted a young man to be his companion, to keep house for him, to sleep in his bed, and be available for sex whenever he wanted.

At the ripe old age of 17, I was feeling the effects of already having spent four years trolling gay bars and oftentimes being with multiple men in one night. I was constantly looking for work, whether it was as a prostitute or even the more normal jobs. I felt like it was time to move on to something that was a larger prize. And I thought being some guy's "wife" might do that for me.

The author was connected with people all over the world. So, he'd take me on trips with him. He loved

49

showing me off as his arm candy. He didn't actually give me a paycheck, but he gave me everything else I wanted. I lived in his house. I rode with him as he drove his Porsche. He bought me really expensive clothes and took me with him to fancy dinners. I was living his life and meeting his needs. He was working on a second book at the time, so he was home a bit more than normal. And when he was home, he always wanted me there with him.

He had a real temper though, and could really be an asshole when he was mad. There was no emotional connection between us. I was an object that he used when he wanted, and if I messed up somehow he would really snap at me. Those were the times that he really reminded me of my father. I put up with it because life with him was better than being a whore. I decided I liked the "wife" part of the arrangement. I liked keeping house for him. I liked not having to worry about earning money. I had time to work on art and photography stuff, and the freedom to cook and do the things that I liked to do.

Then one night he took me to a dinner party at one of his rich buddy's homes, and I met this guy's "companion," Scott. We went out on the deck together to smoke a cigarette... and we ended up having sex. That night started an on-again, off-again relationship between us that lasted the better part of four years and ended both of our "sugar daddy" live-in arrangements.

It didn't take long for Scott and I to decide to make our relationship more permanent. After trying so many other things, I thought it was time to live in a "spouse" capacity with another man around my age. That started the longest relationship of my life up to that point. Scott and I lived together for four years. We had an apartment together, paid the bills together, and did our best at maintaining a long-term relationship. Scott was monogamous with me, but I wasn't with him. I cheated on him a couple of times because I simply didn't have internal boundaries that were strong enough to steer me away from being promiscuous.

This time frame was actually when I first felt some true despair about being gay. I had experienced the gay lifestyle on many different levels... and none of them had worked out for me. I had tried bar hopping and sleeping with a different man every night... and that didn't work. I had tried serving an older man in a live-in capacity... and that didn't work. And now I was in a gay, stable, mostly monogamous relationship... and it didn't feel like that was working either. Here I was in my very early 20s and I had already sampled every stripe of the rainbow that is the gay lifestyle. And none of it brought me any real happiness.

Even though I was barely communicating with my family while in Oregon, I took Scott back to Syracuse with me for a visit over Christmas one year. Actually, my mother's side of the family was lovely to him. And Scott loved my family. Even my father sort of liked him. He hated the fact that he was having sex with his son, but he liked Scott.

Scott golfed. He was not an effeminate guy. He'd worked on a ranch some. He rode a motorcycle and liked playing poker. He'd even had a child with a woman. He was a manly man who just happened to like other men.

51

It bothered me that everyone ended up being so nice to him. Honestly, I had brought him home to force my lifestyle choices on my family and fully intended for the visit to be inflammatory. And then everyone ended up liking him. Though I think that they all still wanted to think he was just my friend and nothing more.

I loved how my being gay was especially tormenting for my father. Not long before I moved to Oregon to live with the author, I was out running some errands with my father. He needed to stop by his office quickly to pick up his paycheck. One of Syracuse's popular gay bars happened to be close to his office. As we pulled up to the curb, two gay guys came out of the bar and walked across the street in front of us. My father muttered, "goddamn fags" and a few other comments about how homosexuals were ruining America.

"I really love how much this gets under his skin," I remember thinking. That thought lodged deeply in me, and honestly it was always running through my mind when I was with a man. My actions always felt like I was, in essence, screaming at my father, "Fuck you! I've got someone else. I don't need anything from you, you asshole."

So the idea of my family - even my father - doing their best to accept Scott and me was pretty deflating. It made me feel like, "oh, they'll just let me live the rest of my life and do this. No one cares." The shock factor was gone and it sort of stripped away one of the core reasons I so deeply wrapped myself in the gay persona.

Chapter IX

I was proudly embracing all of the cultural sides of the gay lifestyle in Oregon when I was living with Scott. I'd howl in laughter with my friends while we chucked condoms at people when taking part in gay rights marches. The AIDS epidemic was prolific then and Ronald Reagan and his Moral Majority were our chief enemies.

By this point, I hated the church. It was a huge, lying piece of crap to me. Taking part in these protests felt cathartic. Like I could scream and jeer and release some of my pent up anger toward my father and my family and the church and all of the ways that all of them had let me down.

I had a few different kinds of interactions with Christians during that time. Some were with people during these marches. You know, the people on the sidelines screaming at us. They brandished signs telling me that I had to stop what I was doing or go to hell. I remember thinking it was laughable for them to try and shame me when they had no idea the shame I already felt. Those born-again types could scream at me all they wanted to tell me there was something wrong with me. I'd just roll my eyes and yell back. There was something wrong with all of us and my sexual behavior was pretty much the least of my problems by then.

All of my contacts with Christians at that time were in the screaming, shaming, "you're going to hell" category except for one. I had a job working in a group home for disabled adults, and the married couple who often worked the evening shift with me were born-again Christians. But they were different than the caricature of the screaming people I encountered during the marches. Joe and Donna rode motorcycles. He'd come in with his leathers and she'd sport a glittery helmet. They were pretty hip and cool, but they were outspoken about their Christian faith. They were the only people of faith who didn't spew shame and accusation on me, even though they were well aware of my lifestyle.

"God loves you right now... do you know that?" Joe said to me one night. "You could turn to him right now and He loves you exactly the way you are."

I had never heard that before so, honestly, I didn't believe him. What he was saying was a total anomaly in the sea of all the negative messages I got from Christians. I dismissed everything he told me about the Lord. It's a shame I didn't give it more thought. Perhaps things might have accelerated more quickly for me.

But other than Joe and Donna, I wanted nothing to do with Christians. Their only goal was to judge me. And I already had more than enough judgment for myself.

Chapter X

I was about 16 or 17 when I first met Jenny at one of my day jobs near the university campus. She was straight, but she went to the gay bars and clubs that I frequented and was constantly hanging out with weird, fringy people. She took an immediate strong liking to me...and as a complete narcissist, I was more than happy to oblige her interest in spending time together. Jenny and I were sympatico from the day we met.

Her father had been a professor at Syracuse University and died when Jenny was pretty young. Her mother had experienced some sort of spiritual awakening and had become a Methodist minister. Jenny had grown up in a parsonage in a rural area and had been treated poorly in the church environment. So we shared this distrust and distaste for Christianity and religion. And now she was finally away at college in the "big city" and was being wild.

I started visiting her in her dorm room and she'd come hang out at my place. We'd talk on the phone a lot and go out every weekend. Other than a quasi-girlfriend that I had for a brief time in high school, it was the first real connection I made with a woman. And it unsettled me.

Jenny and I never had sex, nor did the topic ever openly come up between us. However it sometimes felt like we were a married couple. We definitely fit the stereotype of the gay guy and his straight girlfriend. The two of us grew to be very close. She graduated from Syracuse University a year after I moved out to Oregon, and she decided to move across the country to be close to me again. During the whole period when I was with the rich guy, plus the whole on again/off again thing I had with Scott for four years, Jenny and I were in close contact. In fact, when I needed a place to live on various occasions, I lived with her. Other times, she lived with Scott and me. Jenny was, by far, the most significant woman in my life at this time. During this whole period, I really wasn't speaking to my mother or my sister. My mother had abandoned me, and I lumped my relationship with my sister in with my father issues so I hated her too back then.

So Jenny meant a lot to me. But there was a big problem with our relationship: I was a compulsive liar. And a compulsive manipulator. And a compulsive push-you-away-and-not-let-you-anywhere-near-me kind of person. Not surprisingly, she got tired. I wore her down. Through everything, I believe she genuinely loved me. And deep down, I think I loved her. Or I wanted to.

I would get jealous when she had boyfriends. I truly hated them. I never told her this, but secretly I was jealous of the boyfriends because they were able to be something for her that I wasn't. So I was always really nasty to them. The closer she'd start relating with a guy, the meaner and nastier I would get to her about it.

I'd snap at her and she'd yell, "Why are you being such an asshole about this?" Of course I never told the truth. She just assumed something else and she didn't understand where my reactions were stemming from.

Jenny and I were really close for about four years. But by the end, she finally had enough. There was one relationship she had that turned very serious. I was just mad and angry about it and she confronted me on a bunch of stuff. So I did what I always did... I lied to her face.

She got incredibly angry.

"You know what? There's something wrong with you and I just can't do this anymore. You are not a safe person for me."

She ended up moving out and never spoke to me again until 21 years later.

Jenny's eventual blow-up at me and my complete self-consumption was more fuel for me to really assess how far off track my life was. At first, I really couldn't process what had happened. But once she left, almost all of our mutual friends abandoned me as well. I guess they were waiting for someone to make the first move and were happy to be able to follow Jenny's lead. Some even vocalized the problem. "You know what? Jenny's right. There's something wrong with you and we don't want to hang out with you anymore." It was like we had ended a fake "marriage" and she walked away with our friends in the settlement. I lost nearly every friend I had.

After Jenny left, things were never the same. I completely deserved it. I was a toxic person and made every relationship I was a part of toxic.

I really hurt that woman deeply. But that wasn't something I was considering then. I was just mad at her for abandoning me. It was another nail in the coffin for women with me. Just like when my mother had sent me back to my abusive father, Jenny told me she loved me but didn't act like it – Jenny was just another woman who abandoned me. That whole situation just darkened my soul even more.

Chapter XI

I remember my 21st birthday, sitting alone in a bar because I had basically screwed over all my friends. Honestly, I had no one in my life who cared about me. I had driven everyone away. When the bartender handed me my first drink that night, I blurted out, "It's my 21st birthday!"

He sort of shrugged. "OK..." as he walked away.

It wasn't long after that when it started becoming clear that Scott and I had no real future together. My dream of a wonderful committed relationship was pretty much shot to hell when I couldn't bring myself to be monogamous with him. I was the one who broke things off with him.

Now that I think about Scott from this vantage point in my life, he was a decent guy who was just lost.

But at that point in my life, breaking up with him really sent me into a worse downward spiral. After Scott, I had another brief steady relationship but (no surprise here) it ended when I cheated on him. I had no ability to be loyal. I had no ability to be committed to any type of relationship. In that same vein, I slowly drove all my friends away.

And I started a season of facing the questions about who I was and what I was actually doing in life. If you had asked me at the time, I would have brushed you off while stressing "I'm gay. Leave me alone. I simply haven't met the right man yet. I just haven't found the right setup for this to work." But in retrospect, I can see the deeply unsettling things that were going on. The foundation of everything about me was cracking.

Over the course of my five years in Oregon, I had barely talked to my father. He had remarried during this time, and he moved his new wife into the house where my family had moved to when I was 10.

Unbeknownst to me, my father had gone through a deep depression during that time. After going through some therapy, he started making a few substantive changes... and was actually beginning to soften a bit. He was in his late 40's by this point.

Though he never admitted it to my mother, her leaving him broke him. And when I told him I was gay, it broke him even more. The militant man who tried to control everything about his environment was suddenly in a place where he had little control of anything. It was that breaking allowed a level of self-awareness to creep in. And amazingly, it caused him to start being more thoughtful about his life and relationships.

I didn't know any of this was happening in him. I was busy wallowing and looking for the next man.

Then one day, my father called me.

It was completely out of the blue. I thought something terrible had happened with a family member. But after a few uncomfortable pleasantries, he quietly explained that he was looking to reconnect a little bit.

"You don't sound good," he said after we'd talked for a few minutes.

I nodded...trying to take in where the conversation was going. Then I responded softly, "Yeah, you're right."

"You know, if you ever want to come back home, I'm willing to support you for six months... or maybe a year."

I was silent.

"You'll have to get a job and work on getting your life back together, but I'm willing to help you get some things straightened out."

I hung up without giving him an answer. Now, I had barely spoken to my father for six years, so it took awhile to digest the call. Actually, I thought about it intensely for days. I couldn't shake the thought that something was different about him. He was ... softer. That's the only word I could attach to what my perception was of how he spoke.

A part of me hated how much I despised him, and how much tension and rejection that I forced on him over the years. In some ways, I was treating him in much the same way he had treated me for so long. But now he wanted to connect with me.

And I was starting to think that maybe now I wanted to connect, at least in a small and tentative way, with him.

In retrospect, my father did a really good job with that call. He just had a moment of reaching out....of taking a totally different track than how he had treated me as a child. I had only known him as a man who had cut me off from all things emotional. But with this call, it was like he was trying to appeal to what he saw as the good in his son and not solely focus on what he hated about me.

That phone call really was God's in timing. Jenny's actions, wounding as they were, were a powerful catalyst for me to leave. I was pretty much desperate and at a complete loss for what I should do with my sorry life. I had to be out of my apartment. I had no friends who would help me. I had no man lined up. I was alone and honestly had no idea what to do next. And I was so tired. Just tired to the bone.

When my father called and asked if I wanted to come back, I thought "maybe you just back up and start forward again from where you diverged." So that's why I did it. I didn't really want to go back to Syracuse and be around my family again. But it was tempting to go sleep in his house. Eat his food. And take my time in figuring out what to do next. In light of the unraveling of most things in my life, I thought "What the hell have I got to lose?"

I packed up and left Oregon. And to this day, I have never gone back.

Around the same time that my father called, I started back into more regular communication with my mother too. Well, actually it was her initiation. She called the cops on me one time because I hadn't called her. Oh, it was mortifying. It was early on a Sunday morning and the doorbell rings at my apartment. I had some random man in my bed, and it's the cops. I quickly pulled on a pair of shorts and opened the door.

"Yes, officer?"

"We're here to do a welfare check on you. Your mother asked us to make sure you were okay."

I hadn't called her in a month and she had called me and left a message. When I didn't get back to her, she called the cops and asked them to check on me.

I would go a long time without talking to my mother in that era. I just wasn't communicating with my family a lot because I was out whoring. I didn't think they wanted to hear from me anyway.

But now, here I was on my way back to Syracuse.

Chapter XII

S o I did it. I accepted my father's invitation to come back to Syracuse. I stayed with him a few months - just like he had said when he called me. Just long enough to get back on my feet and at least a little bit re-oriented to East Coast life. Then I moved out into my own apartment that was a just a few minutes from what used to be our family home.

I had to work hard to re-enter family life too. I had been away a long time. After eight years, it was uncomfortable for me to be around family again... even if some of them had made some changes. It was difficult to be around all of the reminders from my childhood. All of that sort of made an unspoken confrontation. "We know who you really are" were the whispers I heard from the familiar surroundings. When I had been in Portland, it was even easier for me to become the fake person that I used to wrap around my wounded soul. I didn't like the reminders that I was just a grown-up version of that little kid from Syracuse. I had liked trying to be this fabulous gay man in this big metropolitan city on the West Coast.

Now, it was harder to hide.

My main relationship at the time was with this really good-looking guy, Will. He was a security guard who was working toward entering the police academy to become a cop. Though we had separate residences, he and I were basically living together. We were sleeping together every night. But there was a different dynamic with Will than what I'd previously experienced: he was two years younger than me. Prior to that, the only thing I had known was being involved with older men. Even though it was only a couple of years different, the psychological effect of it was pretty stark to me... that I was suddenly the older guy dating a younger man. I had a difficult time accepting that fact.

Sure, I was only 24, but I began to feel really old. I had been sexually active for about twelve years at that point. And I had done things in those 24 years that other people would probably take a lifetime to get to. I had a wide variety of life experiences under my belt already - a few good, most bad. I'd traveled a lot and seen a lot of things that most people my age hadn't. My life already encompassed all sorts of outlandish sex. Lots of different drugs. And way too much alcohol.

You know what they say about a car when assessing how much life is left in it - is the mileage city or highway? I had definitely put a lot of "city miles" on my life. I was tired. I felt old. The whole being a young "twinkie" in the gay lifestyle who could pick up any man I wanted had pretty much faded. At least in gay bar standards, I was getting old. I was in my mid-20s. I didn't look like a fresh young kid anymore. I looked and felt like a guy with high mileage.

In all the turmoil, I developed a sleep disorder. I tried everything, medically, spiritually and everything else to try and resolve it. Nighttime would often trigger awful panic attacks. I guess that wasn't a big surprise as I had so many things I was suppressing, desperately working to keep them all shoved beneath the surface. I kept myself busy, almost manic, all the time. I drank lots of coffee. I chain smoked. I desperately tried to distract myself.

But at night when the house got quiet and I was trying to sleep, the distractions faded. This panic disorder severely affected my sleep. It went on for months and crippled me. When it started getting really bad, I started trying to get into bed around 7:30 in the evening just so I could have a reasonable shot at falling asleep by midnight. I would eventually exhaust myself as I took hours to get myself calmed down from the panic attacks.

I lived that way for months. Then one night, I was lying in bed bracing myself for the inevitable panic attack to arise. And I felt somebody sit on the edge of the bed next to me. I don't know why, but I kept my eyes closed, even when I felt them put their hand on my head to soothe me. I fell asleep and slept for like nine blissful hours. I woke up the next day incredibly refreshed and, amazingly, my sleep disorder was gone. Even in my completely pagan lifestyle, I immediately thought it was Jesus who had sat with me that night. I don't know why that was my first thought, but it was. Then I quickly forgot about it and proceeded in my evil pagan ways.

This whole season became increasingly unsettling for me. It had been about a year since I got the surprise invitation from my dad and I moved back from the West Coast. A deep despair had been creeping over me during that whole time and was starting to really settle in. Particularly after the sleep disorder had been cured, I started knowing, deep down, that I was not who I was supposed to be.

And I really began to think seriously about the trajectory of my life. Where was it that I was going to end up? Was I just going to get older and keep dating younger and younger guys? Was I going to turn into being the molester? How young was I going to end up going for... how much was this going to swing? I wasn't attracted to kids or children or anything, but the idea of it scared me. I often thought of those old men at the end of the bar who leer and pick up teenage boys. Was that all my future held?

Incredible loneliness started to envelope me too. Will and I had a good time together, but he didn't really know me. We never really talked on a beyond-the-surface level. I had told so many lies over the years that my family had no idea who I really was. I didn't really have any friends. No one knew me. My existence on this earth felt like it held no value for anyone... especially me.

Chapter XIII

One morning after Will and I had been out the night before, I got up and sort of stumbled into the kitchen. We had been drinking a lot and I was still a bit hungover. Will was getting in the shower as he had to leave for work soon. I started making the coffee.

"Hey, I need to call this guy before I leave," Will yelled out from the bathroom. "Do you have time to look up his number for me quick?" That was back in the days when people still used phone books. I pulled the book out of the drawer and flipped it open. You know how phone books used to have the reference names up at the top of the page – like from *Smith to Smucker*? Or abbreviated down to *Smi to Smu*?

When I flipped open the book, the name at the top of the page that it fell open to was the last name of my sister's boyfriend... my abuser. The first guy I had ever been involved with sexually. I hadn't thought about him for awhile, but suddenly there was his name. It almost felt like it was in flashing lights. And the thought fluttered through my mind... *I wonder what my life would have been like if I had never met him.*

In that moment, I internally collapsed. Everything inside of me felt like a tree that was spongy and rotten, and that "what would my life be like" thought was akin to someone walking by this rotten tree and giving it the shove that toppled it to the ground. There was nothing of substance in me to hold strong at all. A rotten, decrepit collapse was all that I had to show for my life.

With that brief thought, a life-loathing despair enveloped me. It was like being sucked into a black hole standing there in the kitchen of that apartment. Somehow, everything came into sharp focus and I suddenly saw the total nothingness of what and who I was. My life had no life in it. It felt like a complete waste. I was unknown and unloved because nobody knew me well enough to legitimately love me. I was completely invulnerable. There wasn't a single crack in my wall of personal armor. I had worked hard to be totally hidden from everybody. I was utterly, completely, and unnervingly alone.

And a split second after collapsing in that moment of horrifying despair, this presence came into the room. I've described it as an 11-foot-tall invisible Jesus that was suddenly with me in the kitchen. I couldn't actually see Him with my eyes, but in every way, I knew He was there. There was even a weird, sweet, beautiful smell when He appeared. Like a perfect rose, but so beyond what I had ever experienced or enjoyed prior to that point.

My back was to the door and I sensed He was in the doorway. It was this weird spiritual thing, this presence. But weird only in the sense that I can't give a better sensory description. But not at all weird in a way where I felt any fear. This feeling radiated toward me... it honestly felt like a kind of liquid love. It was tangible - tangible enough for me to know that this wasn't some sort of hallucination or anything of the like.

He came from behind me, stepping forward to embrace and envelope me. This presence... this Person... was touching me. Touching the deepest part of me, completely regardless of every emotional wall I had built as an impenetrable fortress. It dove through all the crap and baggage that I wrapped myself in. He went straight to my father wound, that place that I had never been loved and never been touched and never been known. This warm, tangible, liquid love flowed into that spot. And I knew it was Jesus Christ.

I know I might sound like a crazy person, but it's what happened. I remember thinking, "Oh my gosh, those weird Christians were right." (It's funny the things you think in moments like that). And, rather miraculously, I knew that Jesus loved me. And accepted me. And wanted me.

He wanted me.

In an audible voice (this has only happened to me a few times), He said, "You don't have to live like this anymore. I have things I want you to do for me."

I knew what He was saying. "You don't have to live like this anymore." I knew He wasn't talking about the homosexuality. He was talking about my despair. He was talking about my walled-off existence. He was talking about me not being who I was supposed to be.

From my very earliest memories, I had lived an existence defined by a fractured identity and having no idea who I was really supposed to be. Until that moment, I had no idea who I had been created to be. I had spent every day of my life running from even the potential of finding the answer.

My questions had run deep. Aside from simply not knowing what my identity is, I struggled with the very concept of how identity is to be defined. Is it what I choose? Is it what I "self-identify" as? Or is it what God identifies us as?

He spoke to me again. "Your life is a lie and you're meant to be something else. And I'm going to get you there." So I was like... OK. I relented and I accepted what He was saying. And my heart changed. I replied out loud, "I'm going to go wherever you want me to go. And I'm going to do whatever you want me to do."

Even with all the lack of fathering and the destruction from all the men who I had let damage me, I knew that that was the correct way to get what I was trying to get. And that I didn't need anything else but that. Clearly that response is a self-centered motivation, but I was completely bent and misshapen. And that's how God met me – He knew that's what I truly needed to completely draw me away from myself and to Him.

In the background, I heard Will turn off the shower and come out of the bathroom. Moments later, he appears at the doorway wrapping a towel around his waist.

I'm standing with my back against the corner of the kitchen counter, apparently with this look on my face like I was glowing or something.

His eyes widened. "What the hell happened to you?"

71

I laugh even now as I think about my reply to him.
"I've been talking to Jesus."

Chapter XIV

I've shared quite a bit about always feeling like I had led a life that made me feel like I was two different people. From a very early age, I was split by my parents' constant conflict and feeling like I always was forced to choose one of them over the other. It didn't take long for my heart to close off to my father and any influence that a father should have in his son's life. Relatedly, another split happened - as it does for most abuse victims - when they shut down the pain and horror of the abuse and try to live an existence that doesn't show it.

From the time I was 12 when the sexual abuse first started happening in my life, something became truly walled off inside of me and I really just became another person. And I lived with the consequences of that "other personhood" for many years.

So, the moment when I got saved was a powerful beginning of the process to become a whole person again. It was a complete overhaul of the split and allowed me to start living a life of reintegration. If I had to describe it visually, it's a picture of a black cloud hovering over still waters. The still waters represented who I really was and am, but the black cloud was the "other person" I had become that was obscuring the waters. God went down through the black cloud and plunged right into the water. It was the first time something had touched the real me. He wasn't put off by the clouds that obscured me - He just went right through them.

> *I will go before you and will level the mountains; I will break down gates of bronze and cut through bars of iron. I will give you hidden treasures, riches stored in secret places, so that you may know that I am the Lord, the God of Israel, who summons you by name. - Isaiah 45:2-3*

I remember reading the Bible one day and the Holy Spirit really spoke that to me about this verse in Isaiah. "That's me with you. I'm going to cut through all of this crap and all the barriers and I'm going to get at the real you and call you out to be this real person."

Most of my early life, I lived as a liar. Everything about my life was a lie. I didn't know who I was out of ignorance, and then from the ages of 12 to 24, I deliberately created a fake me. But with that artificial existence, I wasn't aware that I was actually creating an impenetrable wall around myself, and then slowly withering and dying behind it.

All along, I lied whenever I had to and never gave it a second thought. I was pathologically and compulsively a liar when I was a teenager and a young adult. I hated conflict and if anyone tried to call me on my shit or tried to confront me about something, I could instantly concoct whatever lie I needed to get out of the moment. And I'd look you straight in the eye while I told you that lie.

I had no connection to reality or truth, which is a primary reason why I hurt a lot of people along the way. I had a few friends here and there, but they always left. And I can't blame them. After a while, they recognized how fake I was, or I inevitably hurt them in an effort to self-protect. They caught me lying to them, or cheating on them in what they thought might have been a monogamous relationship. Or I trashed them to another person and they found out. I had no concept of what real love or real relationships were. I had no capacity for healthy intimacy, for everything in my life was all about me. I was totally and devastatingly self-centered.

But now, being open and honest is super important to me. Telling it like it is is the only way for me to be. I like people who are blunt. I don't like passive aggressiveness. I don't like double entendres and cheeky things. Let's all just put all the fake aside and just be up front with each other.

Prior to meeting Jesus, I wasn't at all aware of the profound effect of my wounds and how I was mismanaging those effects. If anyone got too close or touched the wounds in me, I'd lash out. I would push them away, or lie to cover it, or do whatever it took to ensure they never touched anything in me that was real.

That morning in the kitchen, Jesus just cut through it all like it wasn't even there. After years and years of solidifying a protective fortress around my wounded heart,

He went straight to my core. All of a sudden, it was Him and me. No self-protection. No lies. That's part of why I knew instantly that He was real and He was good. No matter what it took, I wasn't going to let interacting with Him disappear from my life. I was absolutely determined to follow this voice. And I was going to invest whatever I had to in order to build on this amazing new relationship with the Lord.

It's funny, the masculinity of it. The presence felt distinctly masculine to me, even though I don't believe that God is inherently male or female. I believe the masculine and the feminine are both aspects of God's character. But from the start, He interacted with me as a distinctly masculine character, because the deepest aspect of my wound was this lack of connection to my father. Boys need that. Girls do too, but boys need it in a particular way for their identity to be called out.

There was a little boy inside of me whose father never touched him – physically, emotionally, or spiritually. That void left a parched desert place in my soul. But that's the very part of me that this Presence... this Voice touched. It was the first time in my life that I had ever experienced such kindness, such vulnerability, such intimate love. Jesus dove deep through the black clouds and invaded even the most walled off aspects of my life. Suddenly. Immediately. And completely.

God doesn't hesitate to reach into that stuff when He's after somebody. I felt that God wanted me in that moment. I felt that He desired me. There was a moment of imagery for me when God was being a redemptive lover. All my ideas of my warped sexuality coursed through my mind at that moment as I realized that Christ was offering me what I had been chasing after in all those men for all those years.

I had been looking for that deep intimacy, that touching of the deepest part of me – that connection with the masculine and having my own male identity affected.

That's what I got in that split second of time – quite literally. That literal one moment of God touching that one area of me and offering me more was the immediate end of my homosexual behavior. Because He went right to the source of the infection and wiped it out – at a deep fundamental level. At that moment, I recognized that I could only stand to know what was real and made a decision to not pursue the counterfeit anymore.

That's the reason why I never slept with another man from that moment on. The night before that morning in the kitchen was the last time I was ever intimate with a man physically. That type of transformation from homosexual behavior isn't the way it is for everybody. In fact, it's not the norm at all. But it's how it was for me. Boy, when God did it, He really did it. My life, and secondarily my behavior, was fundamentally changed in that singular moment.

I had this incredible deficit in my spirit about the lack of father connection and the lack of connection with other men. A lack of connection with all things masculine. Not

77

surprisingly, this led to my total absence of self-identity as a man.

Something about being sexually intimate with another man seemed to soothe that in me...at least for short windows of time. I craved having that moment of connection. Of union. Of being, at least in some way, one with that person, whatever their image was. For a brief moment, that connection caused my deficit to be overcome.

I was drawn to the types of men who weren't like me at all. I was drawn to straight-acting, muscular men...really the complete opposite of who I was. I can see now that it was really just their masculinity that I was drawn to. That male nature that I was lacking. I craved it, but I knew of no other way to actually connect with it beyond sexual intimacy.

I realize now that other men were utilitarian to me. They were simply a means to an end. A momentary satiating of my craving. My drive to have sex with other men was completely and totally self-centered. I had no interest in wooing or pleasing.

It's almost like "manly men" were my drug of choice. Because in the period of intimacy and for a little while afterward, all that tension that I constantly felt in my spirit would be gone. It was a powerful drug. I simply needed a fix.

But over time I needed more and more. With more and more men. And even with a high frequency of sexual escapades, the positive feeling that I would get each time would grow shorter and shorter.

That's why it's almost like an addiction. At first, it does meet a need and gives you something that feels positive. But over time, you need more and more and it works less and less. Reflexively, you start doing more and more outrageous things to produce that feeling you crave.

Over the years, I had certainly gotten more freakish and more outrageous in my sexual encounters. I constantly lied to people about them. I started degrading myself. Putting my health and safety at risk. Compromising in every way. All just to keep that sexual high going. Because it was the only thing that briefly stilled the storm raging in my mind and in my soul.

That's why the way I met Jesus that morning in the kitchen was so beautifully significant. Prior to that point, I only knew artificial encounters. These guys certainly didn't know the real me. With all of the men, I got a brief hit. Sex somehow let me connect with something that I knew I wasn't. But all of those hundreds and hundreds of sexual experiences offered nothing like the intimacy I immediately sensed God gave me that morning. His presence touched and engulfed the very real and deep need I had for connection. Deep, stable, intimate, and breathtakingly permanent connection.

Certainly the true repair of all of that huge deficit in me came over the next few years. But in the very moment that I met Him, I was overcome with the sense of hope that I was loved exactly the way I was at that very moment. I was no longer trapped and bound by a broken and vacated identity.

Time and sanctification helped me to grow and be a more healthy person as a result of my relationship with Christ. But from that moment of transformation, I was really madly in love with Jesus. He was my brother, my lover, my father, my best friend, my everything. He filled every deficit. He's still all those things to me, but you know how it is when you're first in love. You're nuts about them. You can't stop talking about them. And you think about them 24/7. That's very much how I was as a new Christian. I was just thoroughly in love with Jesus.

Chapter XV

What the hell happened to you? Will had no idea what he was walking into that morning in the kitchen. Apparently the change that came immediately when I met Jesus that moment in the kitchen was visible on my face.

"I'm talking to Jesus," was all that I could respond.

He thought I was nuts. I was changed in an instant. I went from being one person to being a completely changed and different person. All through the amazing work of Jesus Christ.

In time, I ended up getting my own apartment in a crappy Syracuse neighborhood. But I didn't even care — I was in a whole new world.

The first four months after meeting Jesus were unlike any time I'd ever known. The only way I know how to describe it is that I was kind of bathing in the presence of Jesus. I felt this warm, loving presence all day, every day. I would pray and talk to God. And He would answer me sometimes — in my spirit....often through pictures that would come into my mind. Sometimes the Holy Spirit would speak to me. And sometimes I'd even experience that by hearing audible words.

During this amazing four-month period, I knew that I was being discipled and trained by God Himself into a whole new lifestyle of walking in faith. Now I would still go to work and do the mundane stuff like grocery shopping. But mostly, I'd come straight home, sit in my apartment to pray and listen and talk to God. It was an incredible time. But through that whole time, I didn't give the idea of church a thought.

Near the end of that four months, a childhood friend of mine got married. At the wedding reception, I ended up being seated next to a Methodist bishop. We started into the obligatory small talk.

"So, what do you do for a living?"

"I'm a clergyman," he answered.

"Oh? I know Jesus too."

And I started to blurt out all that had happened to me. "Four months ago I surrendered my heart and mind and life to Jesus... He's been changing me and showing me who I really am and what my destiny is and my true identity... " I went on for quite a while.

This kind man just let me talk.

His eyebrows raised at a few points. And he nodded some. Then he sort of cut me off as I kept telling him all that had happened.

"Son, do you have a Bible?

And I'm like... "No. I don't have a Bible."

"Do you go to church? Do you ... know other believers?"

"No. I just hang out with the voice."

Seriously, I didn't know that Christianity had a communal element. Or that it was truly directly based on the Bible. I had been through a decade of pure paganism after growing up with only a culturally-based experience with the church. Truly I had no concept of a spiritual experience being based on Scripture and being fueled by community.

So this man rightly spoke up to introduce me to the church. He told me about a young pastor in his district who was only a few years older than me. "He's a very forward-thinking guy. You should go to his church and tell him that I sent you."

I nodded, hurriedly jotting everything down.

"Here, let me get you a Bible. I've got one in my car. You really need to start reading Scripture."

And, I did.

I ended up making a wonderful connection with the young pastor he sent me to. Actually, I even ended up living with him and his wife for a year or so until shortly after their first baby was born.

Being immersed in a relationship with a mature, male Christian believer was hugely significant for me. This incredibly generous man talked to me. Mentored me. Poured significant time into me. Taught me about Scripture. And got me into church life.

He really got it when I told him about the first thing that God had said to me, that "you don't have to live this way anymore," and that He was offering a way out from a life of despair. Plus, he was on board when I told him about God telling me that "I have things I want you to do for me." This young pastor quickly saw me as having a calling and that, in many ways, I was sort of similar to him. He could recognize from my story that God had saved me for a purpose. That I had a destiny.

After talking through things, he started really encouraging me to think about going to seminary or Bible college, because it seemed like having training and a ministry credential might be important for my future. I'm really grateful that he was able to recognize that in me and nudge me in that direction. His encouragement shaped a lot of things about the new pathway my life would be taking.

That amazing four-month period of unbelievable intimacy with God came to an end. I can really appreciate it for what it was, but I also understand the fact that it was just supposed to be for a season. Getting into community and into the Scriptures was very necessary for me to really start maturing as a believer and as one who would eventually enter into a ministry-based role.

I can still see the look on that Methodist bishop's face... "Oh, I just talk to this voice all day and he talks back" and la la la. Poor guy — he just thought he was going to enjoy some small talk at a wedding reception.

But boy, what a sweet period of romance that was for me and God. Maybe coming out of a gay lifestyle helped me to really understand the Song of Songs, a book in the Bible that highlights the idea of God being our lover. He ravishes my heart. He's jealous for my full attention. He wants to be my first thought. He longs for me to just spend time with Him, sitting at his feet and being fully present with Him.

That initial period in my relationship with Jesus was wonderful, and a helpful preview of what God truly wants from all of us...to be just so centered on Him. I think that type of intimacy and undistracted interaction with the Lord is a restoration of who we're supposed to be and a picture of life untainted by sin and all the crap that the world has done to us. That season was an amazing gift to me, and served as a powerful jumping off point for me to really pursue healing with the Lord.

Chapter XVI

Protection. The power of that word is not lost on me as I consider the natural ramifications that could have come - perhaps should have come - from a decade of unprotected sex with men in the 1980's. In my live-for-the-moment mindset, I never considered how my stupid decisions might impact my life and health in the future. But that aspect is just another reflection of how deeply God cared for me and protected me all along. Here's just one story in that vein.

Back when I was a 16-year-old kid, I was pretty proud of my ability to earn enough money to live on my own. In some ways, it seemed like I had an endless audience of men to earn from. But one night with one man sort of stopped me in my tracks, at least for awhile.

This guy was really aggressive at the bar, being so hot and heavy on me. He'd sit really close and keep touching me, urging me to leave with him. So, even though I thought he was coming on too strong, I agreed to go home with him. A friend of mine stopped me. "Hey, there's something really weird about this guy. You shouldn't go with him."

But I didn't care. I went with him anyway. He was attractive and was certainly my type - really straight looking and acting. There really wasn't much effeminate about him at all. That's the kind of guy who was a real magnet for me.

He was a photographer and told me he lived in this pretty amazing live-work space. Photography was a real interest of mine, so actually I was kind of intrigued to see his stuff. When he heard that, he knew he had me.

He opened the door to his apartment and before I even had my coat off, he had handcuffs unlocked and ready to clasp on my wrists. My friend was right. Something was more off than normal here.

There was a huge pipe running up the wall behind his bed. He cuffed my hands around it, and effectively chained me to this pipe. Slowly, he removed all of my clothing and took a straight razor out of a drawer. Seeing that razor come out really scared the hell out of me. It flashed across my mind - "He's getting ready to castrate me."

Over the course of several hours, he slowly and meticulously shaved me, effectively removing every hair on my body except for what was on my head and my face. With that sharp, straight razor, he shaved everything. My pubic hair, the hair under my arms, everything. I think he was doing his best to make me look as much as possible like a little boy.

Every now and again, I'd see he was aroused while he was shaving me. It wasn't consistent and I wondered why he was so focused. Finally, when he seemed satisfied with his efforts, he got undressed and tried to rape me.

Immediately, he lost his erection. He couldn't do it.

He kept me there all night and well into the next day. He tried to rape me several times. But every single time, he couldn't do it. His erection would disappear. Each time, he got angrier and angrier. I didn't make a sound. I really thought he was going to kill me.

Finally, he gave up, uncuffed me and eventually let me go. I never reported it to the police because I felt like I was complicit in the act. But I called my friend who had warned me and told him that he was right. I was pretty well scared shitless to pick up guys in bars after that.

I found out later the guy had AIDS. In the 1980's, if you were HIV+ or had AIDS, it was the kiss of death.No drugs were around at that point that could control it. Every time I think of that night, I'm stunned and humbled at how God protected me.

When I first became a Christian, I went and got tested for HIV. By that point, I had had sex with more than 1,000 other men, all during the height of the AIDS epidemic. I had been having sex with random men for more than a decade and never used any type of protection. Not once. I thought for sure I had to have been infected with something. When the tests came back showing that I was clean, I could barely believe it.

God showed enormous mercy to me in shielding me from the natural consequences that should have affected me from such a reckless lifestyle. I am incredibly grateful for His protection.

Chapter XVII

After I got saved in the kitchen that day and left Will, there was a brief period where I lived off and on at both my father's and mother's homes. Most of the time I lived in the guest room in the house I grew up in with my father and his new wife. But I was sometimes crashing with my mother and her common law husband, Bob. In that four months, I was primarily just trying to figure out what to do next. My life was swirling with changes and a new way of living after meeting Jesus, but I was really holding on to lots of pent-up feelings about my earthly father.

I remember praying and complaining to God about what a horrible father he had been. And God said to me 'yes, that's true, but you know what? You were a horrible son to him."

I was taken aback. Shocked really... because so much of my lifelong identity had been invested in being a victim and being the poor little boy whose father had ignored him and abused him. Honestly, I had never given a thought to my father's experience with me as a son. Frankly, I've seen many fathers with regimented personalities who have good relationships with their "softer" sons. Why? Because their sons responded differently to that type of hyper-masculine personality. They challenged their father rather than cowering from him. Even in an abusive relationship, there's what happens and then there's how you respond to it. Over the years, I had cemented a particular response to my father.

God continued responding in our conversation, "I want you to be a good son to him going forward. Look at the areas where, as a child, you were a bad son." And I did. I really thought about the areas where I had disrespected him. Now honestly, part of me felt justified that I was a kid and he was an adult. But this is the topic that God took me to.

All of these thoughts were simmering and building up in me to such an extent that one day I just blew up. I was so mad I vomited. The anger that I had been holding in for years and years was really boiling over. I was sitting alone in our family room when my father and stepmother came home from the grocery store. I was standing by the door, red-faced and shaking. My father looked at me puzzled: "What's the matter with you?"

I blurted out the first thing that came to mind.

"WHY DIDN'T YOU COME TO ANY OF MY LITTLE LEAGUE GAMES?"

And I burst into tears. Mary Lou, his wife, grabbed the bag of groceries from him and said quietly, "I'll go put the groceries away — go talk to him."

My dad and I went out into the garage. There was half a case of beer and a carton of cigarettes out there. And the two of us spent six straight hours in that garage. Every hour or two, Mary Lou cautiously opened the door and poked her head in to ask "you guys alright out here?"

My father and I sat and talked for six hours, dragging on cigarettes and drinking cheap beer together. Now, I look back and can mark that conversation as the exact moment I grew up about my father. I got saved in April, and this was probably the July after that. After my conversion, it still took a few months before I was in any type of place to have any type of deep conversation with him.

He asked me point blank: "Something's different. What's going on with you?" I didn't want to talk to him about it, but it seemed like the right time. So, I finally told him about meeting Jesus and getting saved. It felt like such an immense risk for me to be vulnerable with him. But this is where God really walked with me in that conversation. I was so blocked in opening my heart with my father in any real way because of how horrible our past had been together. But that was the day when all that started to change.

We covered a lot of territory in that six hour conversation.

Why did you never come to my little league games?

Why did you make fun of me as a kid?

Why did you hit me all the time?

Why did you.......

Slowly, I let out all my hurt as I posed question after question to him.

And my dad, who had certainly gone through a lot of changes over the time that I had broken off relationship with him.....apologized.

"I'm sorry. I know I was a shit father to you."

I sat back and took a long drag on a cigarette, trying not to seem too stunned.

He told me about his father. Really a lot of things I never knew. My father was born in 1940. My grandfather went off to World War II in 1941 as soon as the bombs dropped in Pearl Harbor. And he didn't come home for five years. He was injured badly and received multiple Purple Hearts. But even beyond the physical injuries, the emotional tumult he went through ended up keeping him in a military hospital in England until the summer of 1946. So, my father, other than knowing that his dad was on the other side of the world being a war hero, did not start a relationship with his own father until he was 6-and-a-half years old. But even at that point, the trauma of war left my grandfather totally emotionally unavailable to all of his children.

I was 24 when we were sitting in the garage having this conversation. And for the first time in my life, I saw my father show some vulnerability and start opening up about our past together.

"You know, honestly, I had no idea what to do. I wasn't prepared to be a father. I had no idea how to raise a kid because my own father wasn't there for me." He told me about how his best friend's father was more of a father figure to him.

Then he started speaking more softly. "And somewhere along the way I got mad and decided to take it out on you. I was frustrated. I was angry all of the time. My marriage was bad. Your mother was constantly fighting with me and spending too much money. I just shut off and ended up being an angry person for 20 years."

I blinked back tears as those words sank deeply into me.

We talked a lot of stuff through that afternoon and evening. I felt like that conversation was what moved me from being subservient to my father to being a man who could look him in the eye as an equal.

He had always been the epicenter of all the hatred and rage I carried. That day in the garage, I just saw him as another man with his own wounding. His own story. His own regrets. I felt sympathy for him. I felt compassion – which I'd never felt for him before. He wasn't a monster to me anymore.

I felt this identification with him because I realized that he had struggled with his identity too, and had failed. Especially with parenting and with his marriage to my mother. It was really a God-ordained healing moment for me. At the end of that evening he hugged me. And he told me he loved me. It was a quiet history-making moment for the two of us.

That was close to 30 years ago now. From that point on, my dad and I have built a friendship over the years and it got better. I'd say he and I are quite good friends now. That conversation was truly a turning point in my life of rebuilding and reforming my relationship with him. Now, he's still who he is. He's a very shut-down, non-emotive person. He's not warm. He's still very Irish and has the classic tendencies that lots of military kids have. But he's open to me in a way that he never was when I was a child.

My dad never did give up on me. He never did. I recognize that now. He couldn't deal with me sometimes and was glad that I was on the other side of the country for lots of years. But anytime I showed any openness or showed any willingness to be positive or forward, he opened the door to me. He never shunned me or pushed me away as an adult.

It's really a great gift to have had that opportunity with my father. Many men who were damaged don't get that type of conversation. They work it out with God and get healing through the church and with other men and stuff. But I know it's rare that it actually gets done with your actual father. I know enough from all of the healing ministry and therapy that I've served in over the years that a restored relationship with my father has been a profound gift to me in my adulthood. I credit his ability to look at the past and discuss it and own his shit with me, and then ask to move forward. He really humbly asked that day, "There's nothing I can do now – it's over. But can we move forward in a different way?" He really asked that. And that unlocked something very deep in me. God really orchestrated a healing moment.

As my identity was being formed when I grew up, my father had always been a non-entity in terms of serving as any type of role model for me. I wanted no part of me to be anything like any part of him. But part of the big change in my personality and manhood after that afternoon in the garage was my cracking the door to being willing to see him in me. Because parts of me were actually like him... and are like him. But, up until that point, I would never admit that consciously because it was too terrible for me to be anything like my father.

I had always felt good about taking after my mother's "eat, drink, and be merry" artistic, ultra-loving family. But honestly, when the going got tough, I watched them all stick their heads in the sand. I didn't do that. I have a strength and perseverance. I'm super loyal and have a strong sense of duty. That's from my father. They're all things from his side. Good, solid people make up my dad's side of the family. They work hard at their jobs. They raise their families. They serve their country and they don't bitch about it. I see aspects of that in me as I've matured into an adult. And as I glimpse in myself some resemblance to him and his family, I'm really grateful for that contribution in my life.

After all this, there's something good and strong about my father that I now accept and embrace. And I accept as God's gift for me. That was another thing that God really impressed upon me early on as a Christian. "You've spent your life pointing your finger at your parents and blaming them for everything that's wrong with you. There's a reason why they're your parents. There's a reason why those two people were the ones who I appointed to care for you. I was the One who picked them for you." So that set me off on this journey of halting the blame game and, instead, looking for God in them. Yes, yes all that shit

95

happened and all of the bad stuff and all of the mistakes. But somewhere in the midst of all of that in my childhood, there's also the story of God shaping me through my parents. That's the story I began earnestly searching for as I started to mature spiritually.

Chapter XVIII

A s a teenager, I fancied myself as a gifted painter. Fortunately one of my high school art teachers was kind enough to tell me that my paintings actually sucked. I think painting might be my old man job though....I want to pick it up again after I retire. I'll paint, and take a ceramics class at the community college and be crotchety.

But that same honest high school teacher encouraged me to try photography. I first picked up a camera when I was 15 - and it turned out I was sort of a natural with it. After I was done making money off of sex with older men, I tried to turn the skill into some money on the side to supplement my other jobs.

After I returned to Syracuse and just a few months after I got saved, I went back to school for photography. My father suggested that I call the local newspaper to ask if someone would be willing to critique my work and give me a few pointers. The photo editor gave me a few minutes and looked at my work, and then ended up hiring me. I was assigned to the advertising bureau at the paper and started taking lots of commercial photos for them.

That new job really fueled my interest. I became an obsessive photographer...I was constantly documenting everything around me. I have some amazing photos of parties in the 80's that could be album covers. I started offering a service of following people for a day to document their life in photos. But even though I was getting pretty good at my craft, I became convicted that this path was wrong for me. God showed me two reasons why He wanted me to give up photography at that point:

1) I was obsessed with reducing people to a moment. I was ignoring a person's real and full story to capture a moment. And that was fueling a dysfunction in me.

2) I was using my camera as a mechanism to let me be around other people, but remain detached and not truly present with them. I was documenting but not interacting. The camera was a safety shield that I was depending on to keep me from relating in a healthy way with others.

God very clearly asked me to stop pursuing photography. I could have gotten a full scholarship to the Newhouse School at Syracuse University. The newspaper's photo editor was shocked when I quit. And my father was disappointed and confused at my decision. But God asked me to give it up, so I gave it up.

I had more of an inkling of what my career path was turning into, though, while on one photo assignment for the paper. Since I worked on the advertising side, I was usually shooting for the weekly glossy insert of car ads and real estate. But every now and again, something big would happen and they'd need me to go out and cover something. I was sent to get some shots of a bad car accident. I dutifully took the photos, but then ended up sitting on the curb with one of the women who was involved in the crash. I probably talked to her for an hour, listening as she cried and poured out her heart to me, and praying for her.

When I got saved, God had said to me, "You don't have to live like this anymore – I have something I want you to do for me." So from that, I had an inkling that some type of ministry would be in my future. But I didn't think it would be in a professional capacity. I thought I might be a godly photographer who had good conversations with people. But that car accident changed my mind. Now, I knew that my skills in ministry were pretty paltry compared to how much I was improving in photography. But God was laying out this path for me and I knew I needed to start taking steps on it. I was pretty scared at this prospect, but I think He likes to throw me into situations where I'm forced to depend on Him. It started to become clear that my calling was in ministry. I was scared, but I knew my destiny was in influencing people.

I transferred the college credits I had accumulated in photography to a small Christian college in southwestern New York state, and started as a full-time ministry student there. College was an incredible time of social re-adjustment for me as I figured out how to have normal male friendships and dipped my toe in the dating pool, even though most of the women there were a good eight years younger than I was. But the academic end of college for me was just as life changing. I declared a double major of Bible and philosophy. I just couldn't get enough of the academic stuff - I dove deeper and deeper and couldn't wait to keep learning more. I studied church history, ancient Greek philosophy and theology all at the same time. At age 29, I graduated summa cum laude with a double major, and as a senior honors scholar for the school's Bible program. Being in a challenging academic environment really just set my heart on fire.

Chapter XIX

As I write this, I am the executive director of a clinical counseling ministry with therapists who offer help for those dealing with relational and sexual issues. I was drawn to this type of service because counseling has ended up being a significant piece of my healing – especially for the first three years after Christ so radically changed my life. It seemed obvious to me I needed the help of a professional therapist to help me work through my narcissism, my emotional immaturity, the sexual abuse...basically all my PTSD stuff. That guided assistance was not unimportant.

But because homosexuality is a relational disorder, the lion's share of my healing came through relational solutions. The most significant healing relationships for me were found in my everyday interactions, like with other men in the church, or the group of guys I hung out with in college.

One of the most impactful early relationships I had was with the pastor who graciously invited me to live with him and his family for a year. I had front-row opportunities to watch him be a wonderful husband and father. It was a great privilege to live in their house and watch his marriage in real time...even when they fought and then worked it out. I had never seen the process of healthy reconciliation modeled before. My parents only had unresolved conflicts. In this pastor's home, for the first time I saw a Christian man and woman getting angry, resolving conflicts, and loving each other through every challenge.

They were just being generous and kind to me to give me an opportunity to live with them for a season. They certainly had nothing to gain from me being there. If anything, it was probably stressful for them to have this wacky kid in their home who had just come out of this alternative lifestyle. But their graciousness helped to change me. It was incredibly valuable for me to have a chance to view a healthy family relationship play out in real life.

Another important relationship was with my friend, Tom. We were house mates at college during the school year and over the summers. Then when I graduated and moved out to California to work after college, he ended up getting a job there too. So we remained house mates all the way up until Gina and I got married. And we're still close friends now, even all these decades later.

These kinds of healthy connections are so restorative. They're just incredible examples of God's grace. Paid professionals can only do so much for people with sexual disorders in helping to deal with addictions, codependency and the like. Real, God-ordained healing requires the church to step in and love these people appropriately, model behavior, and simply be gracious and care. That's really what it boiled down to for me.

Part of the process was me "unclogging my pipes" by getting rid of all sorts of emotional junk, that was key in resolving the pain and indifference I had after being so shattered. That's where the work with the therapist was helpful. Equally important in my healing was being surrounded by people who just loved on me, while being caring, balanced and respectful. It was hard for me to believe that there were people who could authentically and simply care for me, while not taking advantage.

I think of the generous man at church who just met with me once a week for about two years. It really mattered to me that he wasn't paid to be there. He just cared about me. That kind of simple generosity was the thing that brought my heart alive. It was important.

For people who are exiting the type of lifestyle that I had, I absolutely believe that clinical counseling is a crucial step toward healing. And it's best to incorporate that early in the healing process. But for people to really and permanently move away from these types of relational disorders, they must have a stable, healthy church family surrounding them. Real change comes from having a network of people who are godly, respectful, boundaried and willing to just be gracious and loving. Otherwise, the ongoing change just isn't going to work. It's not enough to just extricate all of the relational hurt and garbage. Getting rid of it is just one step on the path to becoming fully functional.

> *"I will make all your enemies turn their backs and run. I will send the hornet ahead of you to drive the Hivites, Canaanites and Hittites out of your way. But I will not drive them out in a single year, because the land would become desolate and the wild animals too numerous for you. Little by little I will drive them out before you, until you have increased enough to take possession of the land."* - *Exodus 23:27b-30*

I remember being really frustrated with God about how long this whole "cleansing" process was taking. I impatiently prayed, "let's get on with it. You TOLD me You have plans for me. I want to know what they are and I want to get rolling."

Not long after that, He took me to the Exodus passage. As a new Christian, my first reaction to this passage was to take it as a promise that, if I followed God, He would bless me and my succeeding family line. While that's part of it, His bigger point to me was to emphasize that this journey I was on was going to be a long process. Not because He was interested in drawing it out and making it more painful than it needed to be, but because the best way to undo all of that needed undoing in me was slowly and carefully. To change too quickly would not be beneficial for me. I wanted the proverbial "magic bullet," but God was much more interested in having me walk on a journey with Him through it.

Around this time, I remember a therapist telling me, "You're about 95 percent anger inside right now. If God took it all away at once, there wouldn't be anything left." That was really true. I had to be built up and braced for a while before the nastiness (which was effectively propping up my emotional foundation) could be replaced.

By this point, I had also made first-hand observations of the concept of relapse. For all of the years that I spent wrapped up in twisted behaviors, it was scary to deal with the overwhelming temptations and inner cravings that would sometimes almost compel me to swing back into old habits. When old habits and patterns are so deeply engrained, the desire for change can evaporate. Some people who are very new to faith are like seeds that sprout up quickly and bloom a bit, but then - just as quickly - wither and die because their root systems have no depth. I was acutely aware of the tremendous weakness within myself and the compulsions that whispered to me to return to my harmful way of life. But Jesus hadn't offered this massive change in direction for my life just to watch it disappear. So, I doubled-down and determined that I was not going to let the new life I was experiencing in Him wither away. Plus, through the authentic relationships I had with other believers, I could observe that there was indeed depth and power that comes with a true relationship with God. There was absolutely no value in me returning to a life built on anger, self-protection and a false foundation. Faulty doesn't work. Fake doesn't work. It's that simple. I experienced both and both failed me. I wanted what was real. It was too important to me to step forward into my faith as authentically as possible, and not be trapped behind any more self-imposed masks. I had spent far too long doing that.

Along with relapse, another thing I was mindful of at the time was displacement. I saw Christians with big, old egos announce that they had given up drinking...but then became obsessed with food. Or people who "overcame" sexual dysfunctions simply by becoming addicted to television as an avenue for checking out from reality. I came to very well see God's wisdom in taking the process slowly for me. I wanted REAL change and REAL recovery and to live a REAL life, not one where I changed just enough to become socially acceptable. I knew it was crucial to really get to the root of what was driving my messed up behavior and offer it up to God, believing that He wanted to make it what it was supposed to be. I didn't want to be changed or just different from who I used to be. I wanted to be the best version of who God had created me to be.

The process was slow. And painful. And arduous. But that's the only way that real change happens in any of us.

As I write this, it's now been about thirty years since I was saved. And the transformation process is still going on in me. I may have had what some term a 'magic bullet' moment that led to behavioral change, but that was followed by years of healing, prayer, counseling, mentoring, spiritual direction, tough choices, and feeling horrible things that I didn't want to feel and had buried for years. It required letting go of a lot of pain. It required letting go of my narcissism.

Have you ever heard someone talk about it taking ten years to become an "overnight success?" It's the same sort of idea with my healing. It was a magic bullet moment that could only work in conjunction with a long process. And that process is still evolving in me, even thirty years later.

Chapter XX

In my first few years as a new Christian, I had the privilege of having a few older men in more of a "fathering" or mentoring role with me, rather than a peer relationship. One man, in particular, met with me every week at the local Denny's for coffee. He didn't do it because the church asked him to or because he was being paid to. He just liked me and wanted to see me grow and succeed in life. I really owe a lot to that man. He affirmed and shaped a lot of my character, and blessed me a lot in that year or two when we met together regularly.

My time as a non-traditional college student also afforded me life-changing opportunities to have healthier relationships with male friends. I came in as a non-traditional student who was a good eight years older than my other freshman classmates. I was given the option of living off campus rather than having to live in a dorm, so I ended up living in a house not far from campus with seven other guys.

All of these guys had either just graduated from college or were seniors when I was starting, so the age difference wasn't as great. Living in that all male fraternal environment was hugely helpful to me. With years and years of nothing but unhealthy, broken relationship with men, plus little experience in defining healthy relational boundaries, most of my life was spent completely devoid of good male friendships. God was gracious to put me in this living environment so that all of that could start to change.

I did have one bad male friendship that ended during this time. He was the first guy who I became friends with post-conversion, but it was just unhealthy. It didn't take long for me to become pretty co-dependent on him. My identity just wasn't solid enough yet. I hadn't shaken all of the old behaviors and patterns yet, and that left me tempted to eroticize him and other stuff. I refer to him sometimes as a "dry drunk" friend. There were still some aspects of possessiveness, poor boundaries and jealousy in our friendship ...in the same manner as they would show up in a homosexual relationship. But we were never physical with each other.

I felt like a huge failure, but I was determined to learn from it. That misstep helped me to realize that part of being a healthy man is being capable of having boundaried, respectful relationships. Men very much respect other men's boundaries. We don't violate each other. And eroticizing another man, even if he's unaware that it's happening, is a big-time violation of boundaries. Learning the ropes with that whole topic was really important for me in that season.

In that failed friendship I did end up working a little of that stuff out, but I ultimately pulled away from him and ended our relationship because I recognized the misshapen emotional dependency that I had toward him. There would be no success in that friendship for me until I made some major changes.

Getting in to college was great because there was a whole bunch of different guys for me to get to know. It was far less tempting to just fixate on one. I could just experience the wonderful freedom of being in a group of men, but not being "stuck" to any one of them. Respectful and boundaried. Each of us contributing our own individual dynamic to the group. We could each have fun without the need to cling to each other. It was a tremendous dynamic for me to experience.

It didn't take long for one friend from that group to really start re-shaping my need for a male peer friend...in a good and healthy way, though.

I was a double major in college, Bible and philosophy. Another guy in the house where I was living was a rec major. Honestly, the first time I met him I didn't like him at all. He was younger than me, maybe by five years or so, and he rode a motorcycle. I just thought he was a dick. The first time I went back to Syracuse on a long break from college (it was about a three-hour drive), this guy called me out of the blue and said "I gotta get out of town. This town is driving me nuts. Can I come stay with you for the break?" I was like "uh... OK." So he came and stayed for quite a few weeks. And we became friends from then on out.

It was interesting, God spoke to me about him not long after that semester break. I remember that there was something about him that was irritating me and I was talking to the Lord about it. And the Lord said, "You and he are going to be friends until one of you dies."

"What? That one? Out of all the people I know, that one?"

But I know it was God who gave me Tom as a friend. The group dynamic of friends was great, but He allowed me to build on a significant, boundaried, healthy, close male friendship to bind up more of my wounds.

To be honest, when I first met Tom, I was tempted to eroticize him because he tripped my "other" switch. He seemed to be so much more masculine than I was at the time, and there was an impulse on my part to fear him a bit, but also secretly desire him. God helped me to keep those feelings in check and work through them as our relationship grew in a healthy manner.

Tom's always been kind of a gregarious guy...very friendly and extroverted. We've long joked that he should run for political office as he's glad to shake hands and kiss babies. He really called out of me an outgoing and easy-going nature that I simply didn't have prior to meeting him. We played poker with groups of guys. We went bowling. I'd be holed up in my room studying and he'd knock on my door and drag me out - "come on, we're going to go get wings." He taught me how to relax and not always take everything so seriously.

But he could be serious when it was needed. I broke up with a girlfriend once and he stayed up with me one night and talked me through it. It was just a really good, brotherly dynamic. I've thought about how my life might

111

have been different if I would have had a brother growing up to serve as another male influence in my childhood other than my father. I've asked God about it. Who knows. But in my late 20's, God was giving me a brother figure to call out that new dynamic in me.

Out of all the groups of guys and all the friends that I ended up making, Tom has always stood out to me... in part because of what God said to me about him, but in part because I really respected him. He made it easy for me to grow to admire him without eroticizing him and wanting to "be" him. I know he never had those feelings toward me. He doesn't go that way, never did. He's always been someone who was pretty emotionally healthy and had a good sense of his own identity as a man. It was definitely a help to me in shaping my new sense of male identity to have such a good connection with a guy who was comfortable in his own skin. Everything about the establishment of our friendship was boundaried and respectful. I had never had that before - he's the archetype of something for me. There was something profoundly very "male" between the two of us that was such a positive influence for me at that point in my life. Tom was the best man in my wedding and he and his wife often come to visit my wife and my family. All these years later, we're still best friends. He feels like a childhood friend that I grew up with, even though I didn't meet him until I was 26.

Tom and I often joke about how much I made it clear that I hated him early on. I don't think he even knows the level of importance he was in my life, because we're guys and we don't talk about that kind of stuff. But God certainly established a life-changing dynamic for me when this friendship was forged. And I'm very grateful.

Chapter XXI

After graduating from college, I was offered a scholarship to attend a seminary in southern California. But after consideration, I didn't accept the scholarship and instead moved to Watts, CA (near Los Angeles) to start a job with an inner city ministry. The college girlfriend I was most serious about lived in San Leandro, CA, a town in the Bay Area. I figured that we could hop the train and still see each other pretty regularly. I wanted to pursue this because for the first time in my life, I felt like I'd met a woman who I might actually want to marry.

But two weeks before my job started, the group that had hired me decided to switch me to San Francisco instead. So rather than being five hours away from each other by train, we would now be living and working in the same city. This location change really caught me off guard, so I took that as a sign that I was to marry Catherine. We had been talking about the idea of marriage for awhile, so I went ahead and bought a ring. But no matter what, I just couldn't shake the gut feeling that proposing to her would be the wrong move. I wrapped the ring and its box up in tin foil and put it in my freezer. It wasn't time to move ahead yet.

She was eight years younger than me, but that difference wasn't an issue for either of us. Our values, our lifestyles, our likes and dislikes...they all fit together quite well. Except for one big thing - Catherine didn't want children. At the very least, she didn't want to have children for a long time....but we both knew that it was very likely that she didn't want them at all. Once we got to the point of truly deciding about our future together and it got to be ground zero in considering what our joint destinies were to be, I just couldn't really reconcile my life not including fatherhood. By this point in my life, I knew it was a major calling for me to have kids and to raise a family.

We faced the type of divergence that is a deal breaker for marriage. After two years of dating and establishing a significant bond with one another, we took a month-long break to pray about what we should do. At the end of that time, I broke things off with her because I believe the Lord had spoken to me to do so. We cried and held each other and hugged while we said what needed to be said. We both acknowledged that we really loved each other and really were good for each other. But we acknowledged together that, for whatever reasons, God was saying no to the future of the relationship.

Catherine was mature enough to have that discussion. She wasn't petulant and angry. Instead, she was able to make a deep and understanding acknowledgment ... "You're right." We didn't fight, we weren't mad at each other. And honestly, that made the emotional break of it harder. I just knew in my gut that I wasn't supposed to marry her.

It's interesting – when Catherine and I broke up, she went to grad school and has become a really successful therapist in northern California. She's had an amazing career working with at-risk youth who've been abused and otherwise traumatized. An amazing career that I would have probably denied her if we'd married and I had steered her toward a more ministerial or domestic role. Had she married me, Catherine would have missed her destiny and not become this phenomenal healer she is now. And she would have denied me the destiny of becoming a father. I couldn't see all of this at the time, but I can certainly see it now.

While Catherine and I were getting close to our final decision to end things, I got angry. Actually, I was really mad about not being in L.A. I wanted to be in L.A. and do inner city cross-cultural racial reconciliation for my job. Before my new employer switched my job to L.A., I would have been in Watts, where the historic riots in 1965 happened. At this point, it was the late 1990's and there was plenty of stuff happening in that area again. I wanted to be there - which is kind of nuts because there weren't too many white people who were angry about not being put in that area. But now I'd been shifted to Oakland and thought it was because I was supposed to get married. And now that plan was shot.

In my mind, God had messed up everything by having me end up in Oakland. And I was pissed off. I was up on the rooftop of where I lived, basically yelling at God about not giving me what I wanted. Oh, I was such a selfish little shit at that age.

Chapter XXII

While I was nursing my wounds from the end of that relationship with Catherine, my friend had a feeling about another woman that he knew. He talked to me about her on a few occasions and thought we'd be a good fit for each other. This lady, Gina, was living in Italy and serving with a missions organization there after completing Bible school.

A few weeks before she came home on furlough, he tossed me a photo of Gina.

"Look... Gina Tucci. She's actually coming home soon. You should meet her."

I looked at the picture. "Nah, she's not my type." And I threw the picture back at him.

It wasn't long after that that a group of my friends hosted a dinner party. It certainly wasn't a high-brow affair. It was a whole crowd of people crammed into this tiny apartment, with little room to move around. And there across the room from me, I saw Gina standing next to a faded old, loveseat.

I weaved through the people to get closer to her, and we both moved to sit down at the same time. I looked in her eyes and smiled... and I just knew. I knew. I know it's completely cheesy to say it that way, but I knew that I was going to marry her. Screw "not my type."

Something happened in my spirit — I feel like I just fell into her eyes. Certainly that sounds schmaltzy, but I've never been able to come up with a better way to describe it. I knew I was going to marry that woman before she even said one word to me.

It's interesting that Gina says that she had the same type of reaction that evening. She spied me from across the room, sort of crammed over by the door of the apartment. Trust me when I tell you that I was not her type. At the time, I was rail thin (oh, to be young again), about 130 pounds with long, unkempt hair pulled up in a ponytail, and a goatee. I think the look I was going for at the time was some sort of combination of drug dealer, Latino, and Jesus freak, with the ensemble tied together with a raggedy flannel shirt and dusty Teva sandals. She will laughingly tell you she had zero physical attraction to me at all. And then she felt like God said to her, "This is for you. This is who I have saved you for."

This beautiful woman was a 31-year-old San Francisco native. And she was saving herself for marriage. I still think it's unbelievable that she grew up in the 1970's in the city in America where most anything in the sexual arena was not only accepted, but celebrated. But there she was that evening...a fervent, beautiful, Christian virgin in her early 30's, who had been serving in Italy but was now back in San Francisco. And God had just given her the sense that she was looking at the man for whom she had been saving herself.

We talked until 2 in the morning that night. It turned out she was half-Italian like me. We even had pretty similar family backgrounds. It was kind of amazing how much we had in common. And then she told me she was actually engaged to a guy, Benino, in Italy, or "promised" as they refer to it there. I gulped at first, but honestly, it didn't bother me that much. I had that kind of confidence, even on the night we met, that God was going to bring us together.

Before going to bed that night, I went up on the roof and looked up at the sky - the same rooftop where I'd been yelling at God just a few nights before. I prayed, "God, I don't know how you're going to work all this out, but thank you for Gina."

Because I knew He had done this, I knew somehow it was going to work out. I had a bedrock confidence. She could go ahead and reject me. I didn't care. I knew it was going to work out.

It turns out that Gina was in a similar type of situation that I had recently been in with Catherine. Benino had asked her to marry him – and she had even met his family as his impending wife, as per Italian tradition. But, she just wasn't sure. Her gut was telling her no. She was using these couple of weeks while being home in California on furlough to think through whether she really wanted to marry him or not.

I absolutely was not expecting Gina. I was over 30 and had pretty much given up on the idea of finding someone after Catherine. But then we met next to a dusty loveseat in my friend's apartment, and I just knew. And Gina had this confidence that God was saving her – then she looked up at that crowded party and saw this skeevy guy across the room and heard God say that to her about me. And (sort of understandably) she was afraid. She was nearly engaged to another guy.

But a few weeks later, she flew back to Italy and dumped Benino. When she came back, I excitedly asked her out on a date. "No," was the rather quick reply. She realized, like I did, that God had us for each other, but it was just too much for her to deal with then. She needed time to get over her engagement. And time to process. And time to just readjust to being back in the States. She'd been on the mission field and had been considering the rest of her life with a man, and suddenly she's back in the U.S. looking for work and her left hand devoid of an engagement ring.

Actually, her need to wait played in my favor. Women love confident men, because they love to be wooed and chased. And I was confident and ready to chase. I didn't care what amount of time she needed.

As it turns out, we never really dated. We just started doing a lot of things together as friends.

The whole thing with my job in Oakland blew up just a little while after Gina came back from Italy. So I ended up as an associate pastor on the staff of a nondenominational church in San Francisco. It just so happened to be at the church where Gina attended. The job opened up kind of suddenly and the mutual friend who had introduced Gina

121

and me made a call that started the process of me getting the job. That doesn't count as stalking, right?

Gina and I started working on lots of outreaches and projects together. She's a teacher – so we were able to develop a partnership between the church and some of the local public schools. I always found ways to be around her and work with her and get to know her.

There were some distractions. A lot of women were interested in me. And a LOT of men were interested in Gina. We were both in our early 30's, attractive, and single. I was patient with lots of other men sniffing around Gina, but I kept a close eye on her.

After months of all of this time together, we developed a really close friendship. I think that time investment and that close friendship is actually a big reason why our marriage has been so successful. The formulative base of our marriage isn't sex or the kids. Sure, there's romance there, but the base has always been a tight friendship and a shared sense of purpose and identity. We both went through a really deep identity cleansing process with the Lord prior to meeting each other. Because of that, we both really knew who we were ... which set us up to better understand who we were in relationship with each other. There's this real thing, this soul connection, that transcends the physical part of our marriage. It's more than raising kids together and thinking about what happens in retirement. The close friendship we built in those early days has only grown deeper with time.

I met Gina in August. And I remember I kissed her on Valentine's Day. We were up at Twin Peaks in San

Francisco, overlooking the city. It was a beautiful evening. And I just leaned over and planted one on her lips. She pushed me away. "Oh, no, no, we can't do this."

With the level of closeness that we had developed, she knew if we did much more than hold hands we'd end up sleeping with each other. I had been celibate for eight years. And she was a virgin in her 30's who was waiting for marriage. Gina was - and is - a very smart woman.

We got engaged in July. We were sitting in a café, where we met just about every day. Nothing was out of the ordinary. We were just sitting there – she was drinking a Sprite and I had a cup of coffee. I looked at her and, rather matter of factly announced, "I think we should get married."

My timing was a bit poor as she spit a mouthful of Sprite out in her surprise.

"What???"

"I think we should get married," I repeated. I just said it.

And there was this long really uncomfortable pause. And she said ... "Okay."

"Really?"

"Okay."

The whole thing had all been unspoken and under the surface for months. We were so weird. But all throughout that time together as friends, our hearts were really being quietly knit together. It was so obvious at that point – I figured I might as well just blurt it out.

We called our parents and told our friends. Since we'd always been clear that we "hadn't been dating," honestly, our friends were kind of in shock. (Now we joke about it.) But then she asked me to do it properly. So, I went out and bought a diamond ring. She was going back to Italy for a couple of weeks to visit and to pick up some of her stuff that she had left there the previous year. (She was certain now that she wouldn't be going back.) I figured if she going to be seeing Benino again, I should probably get a ring on her finger.

When you cross the Golden Gate Bridge from San Francisco over to the Marin side, there's a huge cliff that's almost as high as the bridge. When you stand on the cliff, you can overlook the bridge and see the whole city glittering in the background. There's one lone tree that sort of stands separately from the rest on that cliff, and it was under that tree that I knelt down and properly asked Gina to marry me. We carved our initials in the tree that night. We have a long narrow picture that's a panorama view of the city – San Francisco, the bay, the bridge. Over in the corner of the picture, you can see the edge of the cliff and that one lonely tree. That picture will always hang in our home.

Gina went back to Italy, gathered up what she'd left there, came back and started planning the wedding. She's half-Italian and half-Jewish, so there were lots of expectations for the ceremony. What was the best setting? A Catholic church? A synagogue? A non-denominational church? There was lots of murmuring. So we just decided to get married in a well-known hotel in San Francisco because it was neutral ground.

124

The ceremony really was beautiful and it incorporated elements of catholicism, evangelicalism and Judaism. I was the guy who had grown up Catholic but I had no problem smashing the glass and dancing to *Hava Nagila* at the reception. We planned to have a *chuppah*, a canopy that Jewish couples typically used in their weddings. But shortly before the big day, God spoke to Gina one night and said "I will be your *chuppah*." So she canceled it. I wasn't sure what it was to symbolize so I looked it up: the canopy symbolizes the tabernacle and spiritual covering over the marriage.

Many of those who attended our wedding ceremony told us that our wedding was different than any other that they had been to. There was something in the room that was palpable. One of our friends who didn't know about the *chuppah* story told us, "It looked like there was this weird thing over you during the ceremony. I could almost see the presence of God over you as you were taking your vows." We nodded, surprised but smiling. The *chuppah* was apparently there after all.

There has always been something very spiritually relevant about our marriage. I really thought we would be teaching together and ministering together in our marriage. We're both the first real Christians in both of our family lineages and, over the years, it's become evident that God is starting a new type of line with us. In the beginning, we'd planned on waiting to start a family. We had all these lofty thoughts of what we'd do together as a couple before having kids. And God was like, "There's someone I want to bring forth from you." So we were only married for seven weeks when Gina told me she was pregnant.

Before I proposed to Gina that night on the cliff overlooking the bay, I knew I had to be clear with her on everything about my past. Everything. She knew bits of pieces of it, not all in context though. We had talked a lot about our childhoods, but had not really touched on many specifics about my complicated sexual history. Boy, when you roll that one out...

She had a vague sense of all the chapters in my story up to that point, but I knew I had to tell her the horror of it all and not gloss over the details. She deserved to know.

I came home from work and she was up on the roof deck of my house. I nervously climbed the stairs and told her, "I really can't marry you unless you know everything about what you're getting into." So I told her everything. I assured her that I'd been tested for anything that would affect us physically - and that miraculously, everything was clear and that she had no need to worry.

But then I emphasized, "I really want you to understand, I'm solid with God now but I've seen how the kind of life I've led... how it affects other people. People go off the reservation. I just can't guarantee you that, over decades, I'm not going to go ... wrong... at some point. I think it's important you understand and fully know what you're getting into." So I really laid it all out there. I didn't want to leave her with any false impressions or give her a rosy expectation that I couldn't guarantee I could live up to.

She listened. Nodding. "I'm in." And that's all it took. Once she made up her mind with me, she'd made up her mind. There was no turning back.

God was beyond gracious to me to connect me with a woman who had no hesitation when she heard about my past. She grew up in San Francisco in the 1970's. She had seen lots of freak show stuff for her entire life....so my freak show past didn't really seem to phase her.

Plus, since we came from similar types of broken backgrounds, she deeply understood all of the context of my story. She grew up in the Italian ghetto in San Francisco. I grew up in the Italian ghetto in Syracuse. She always had her cousins around, just like I did as a kid. Her father had had multiple affairs and her mother had been involved in one as well. She was horribly tormented about some things throughout junior high and high school. She grew up in a broken, chaotic environment. She really had a paradigm that helped her to understand who I had been, and who God was changing me to be. She just latched on to Jesus earlier than I did and had a great, supportive network of friends earlier than me.

When we were deciding to get married, we didn't talk excessively about gay sex or all that I had done. We talked about how I was acting out results of some of the feelings generated in me during the earliest years of my life, and what all my behavior choices had stemmed from. She got why I ended up on that path, and she got how much Jesus had turned me around. My wife is an amazing woman.

Even though I had gone through several medical tests years earlier, I got tested again when Gina and I got engaged. I was truly worried that the earlier tests just weren't accurate. Before I married this amazing woman and pursued having children with her, I absolutely needed to know for sure whether or not I was clean from all disease.

I went to get the HIV test done on a Friday and had to wait through the weekend for the results. I was trying to hide how nervous I was. A guy at my church (who I knew was gifted prophetically and often heard from the Lord) passed me and grabbed my arm.

"I feel like God is saying to you don't worry about it, I took care of it."

I knew he was talking about the HIV test, even though he had no idea about the situation. Still, I couldn't sleep that night. The test results came back on Monday and everything was negative. Amazingly, I was clean.

I thought back to that night when I was chained naked to a pipe in a deranged man's bedroom and marveled again at how I was spared. I wondered if God knew that someday I was going to surrender to him and that my destiny was to have four amazing children and enjoy marriage with Gina.

Did I have a disease at some point and God healed me miraculously? Or, did He orchestrate the men who I was with so that I never contracted anything through all of those years? It would be speculative for me to say. But I've often wondered. All I know is that God spoke to me through this guy - "I took care of it." In spite of my extremely reckless behavior for a decade, God took care of it. There was great mercy for me. And I am profoundly grateful. God's purpose was for me to enjoy marriage and to father children, and He didn't want anything to be a barrier to that. He really gave me a clean slate when I became a Christian... spiritually and even physically.

I remember when I first got saved being faced with the enormity of my wrong choices in life and the sin and brokenness that had defined me up until then. I was really eaten up with regret. Everything in my life seemed so off-track. The friends I had in high school had all gone off and made something of their lives. They were becoming doctors and lawyers, and I was back in my hometown, living in a crappy apartment, and was pretty much just a tired ex-whore.

I had always been pretty smart and did really well in school. In spite of everything that had happened, I knew I had a brain. I had just never pursued anything that led to me living up to my potential.

In this downward spiral, God graciously showed me a line from the second chapter in the book of Joel:

"I will restore to you the years that the swarming locust has eaten."

The nation of Israel was in a similar spot, as they were lamenting everything that had happened regarding the destruction in Jerusalem. The regret in the story was palpable. And God said through the prophet Joel, "I will restore to you..."

God was telling me to stop worrying. "It's going to take some time to catch up but I will renew your life in such a way that there will come a time where you'll be where you would have been had you never acted out." I feel like that happened in my 30's. After everything with my education and meeting Gina and starting our family, I caught up and it felt like I was where I would have been had I not wasted those years from 14 to 24. And God gave me everything that I would have had. Amazingly, God restored   the   years.

Chapter XXIII

L et me just give a clear defining statement: my experience (and I believe yours too) clearly depicts that there is something to the created order that we are innately created heterosexual unless something goes awry. The default setting – the factory preset if you will - on human beings is opposite gender attraction which leads to reproduction. I think that's just how God designed the species. People who feel differently are at odds with something very deep in our created order.

Here's what that also means: because we all bear the image of God, my experience of suddenly having heterosexual ... stuff and reactions wasn't forced. I didn't have to make that happen. It just kind of happens. As I journeyed along in my new relationship with Jesus Christ, definitely by the third year or so, I had begun to change. My affect changed in a distinctively masculine way, and my personality became more direct, forceful and honest.

Women can almost always tell what a man's about when they meet him. In the past, I had always tripped a "sister switch." I was always a buddy and a pal to women and there was a lack of sexual tension in those relationships. I noticed that dynamic began to change when I changed enough to start giving off more of a male vibe. The "sister switch" disappeared and women started to not respond to me as a friend, but instead not speak so freely around me and see me more as an object.

It's strange – I remember sensing that. Women weren't as readily willing to be friends with me anymore. I think a big part of it was I was just giving off that male sense in a way I never had before. And the natural reaction? Women started responding to that in the natural way by treating me as the "other"... something and someone clearly different than them.

I think that gets into the issue of identity. For most of my life, I strongly identified with my mother and had mostly female friends. After becoming a Christian, God started really calling out my identity as a man and as a male. As I started living out that identity and giving out that vibe, women became the "other." That meant sexual tension and attraction. It was different. And it was good.

As I became more competent and secure in my masculine identity, healed from the sexual abuse and untwisted from all the crap with my father, the changes were undeniable.

I remember one day while working at a newspaper in New York. A female co-worker walked by my desk and I looked up and my eyes went right to her boobs. Quite literally, this had never happened to me before. I was a 25-year-old man, but it was the first time I had had that type of moment with a woman.

132

When I looked up, my eyes locked straight on those breasts. It was a little shocking to me that I simply could not make myself look away. I laugh now looking back at this but it was so strange at the time. I just had a moment of lack of impulse control and my eyes kept following her as she walked away. I started to get an erection while sitting at my desk. Oh my, it was just so weird. I knew for sure that whatever kind of regenerated man that I was becoming now wanted to encounter women in a COMPLETELY different way. The "sister switch" days were long gone. And it just kept going from there.

I never had to make my heterosexual stuff come out. I never had to force it or create it. It was there dormant underneath all the garbage and the yuck. As my healing deepened, it all just started to become uncovered.

Just because the physiological changes were happening didn't mean I had the emotional maturity to keep up with them, though. My dating journey started and I guess I tried to make up for all the time I had lost. I dated a lot of women in a pretty short window of time. Even after I became a Christian, I was still extremely narcissistic for quite an extended season. I was not used to being "other centered"...it was far too natural for me to be totally self-focused. I had only known relationships that were completely driven by what my needs were.

Slowly, the Lord had to use dating and women to call a genuine care for others out of me. He also used some significant male friendships to help me see my selfishness, and to learn what to do in a normal, healthy dating relationship.

I dated a lot before I met my wife. I took each of those relationships as a learning experience, gleaning a bit more with each one as to how to rightly relate with women. God dealt with all of this congruently in me. As I became healthier, women truly became the "other" to me and normal sexual attraction happened...on my part and on theirs.

Chapter XXIV

In college, I was a complete idiot with women because, emotionally, I was a 13-year-old living in a 24-year-old's body. Since you can't just skip over developmental steps, I had a lot of bad experiences where I just didn't do the right thing and ended up hurting some women. As I was trying to find my footing as a straight adult man, I was, unfortunately, pretty careless with women's hearts for a few years. I dated a lot. I would break up with a woman and have another girlfriend within two weeks because I was viewing it like a training exercise.

At this point, I knew God wanted me to get married and my eyes were fixed on the "wife goal." I knew I needed to understand women as a straight man and I (immaturely) thought the only way to learn was by immersing myself in relationship after relationship. I was an aggressive dater and had lots of different experiences with these women. Every time I failed, I did learn from it and did my best not to repeat that particular mistake in future relationships. But in my immaturity, I didn't do a good job of caring for these women's hearts in the process. Resultingly, there are a fair number of women who would probably roll their eyes if my name would come up. But they all taught me something. All of these casual relationships built my confidence to enter into a serious relationship with Catherine, and then, eventually, an engagement with my wife.

After all of the rather manic dating I was doing, there remained a significant obstacle between my heart and marriage: simply trusting women. I couldn't shake the feeling that my mother's betrayal had sunk deeply into me. She spent much of my childhood talking with me about the day we were finally going to get away from my father. Then after living away from him for a couple of months, she sent me back to him because she wanted to date wildly and be free. My mother was the only nuclear family member that I had received any type of unconditional love from, so when she sent me back to my father... it was awful. For a few years, she was seemingly dead to me. I remember telling her, "You just betrayed everything since I was a little boy. You just betrayed our entire story... for yourself." So by virtue of her actions, I had closed myself off emotionally to all women.

God was the one who had to deal with that in me. Since I was so clear on the fact that He spoke to me that I would be married, I had to squarely take on that distrust. That's a big part of why I was so squirrelly in all of those fast and furious dating relationships. Relating with women like that was dredging up emotions....but God used those

136

experiences to slowly peel away at the scar and start to bring healing.

The eventual deep healing process that the Lord brought me through with my distrust of women left me with two huge assets when I married Gina: the bravery to leave those mistrust issues in the past, and the willingness to enter marriage open-hearted and with no secrets. I can honestly say I completely trust my wife. I don't worry about her. I'm not jealous of her. God gave me such an unshakable confidence about Gina and I being together that any of those nagging doubts evaporated.

Chapter XXV

There was eight years between that day in the kitchen and the day that I married my wife. I was celibate that entire time.

Very early in my walk with the Lord, I took two vows: that I would be chaste until marriage, and that I would live a life of simplicity. I would go through life not taking more than what I needed. That I would be happy with "enough." That I would not always need bigger, larger, better, newer. I saw the trap that came with constant want. I had lived through the trap. I had seen it with my parents, with their ungodly attachment to money and material growth. I knew that I wanted to circumvent that in my own life, so I took these vows of chastity and simplicity.

I did, indeed, keep my vow to be chaste until I got married. So my first experience with real sex was with my wife on my wedding night at 31 years of age. And let me just say that the difference is almost beyond my ability to explain.

My perspective certainly covers a very wide spectrum of experiences. After years and years of pagan sex with more than a thousand men, I was now enjoying sex in the manner as it is defined in the Bible: with one committed, monogamous spouse of the opposite sex.

Prior to marriage, the only sex that I had known was incredibly self-centered. Gay sex, for me, was completely self-centered. It was about these men meeting a particular need in me and fulfilling something that I needed them to be. Each man was just an object. Each time I slept with a man, he was just my drug of choice for that moment. These men just met a craving...and over time they turned into what I needed to get through the day and to just survive.

It is a totally and radically different experience when two whole people come together with God's blessing. The empty connection I desperately sought with each of those men just has no comparison with the type of spiritual connection I have with my wife physically. For one thing, I get lost in it. Even after 20 years of enjoying sex with my wife, I still get lost in it. It's one of those creative experiences with God's presence where you just lose all track of time in what you're doing.

Married sex is a spiritual union that's far beyond the physical union. It's a connection unlike I've ever felt with another human being. My wife is not an object. What she gives is not a drug that gets me through until the next hit. We are two whole people coming together and mutually surrendering to each other. It's a beautiful opportunity to serve each other.

I'll just add that God really liberated me from the hangups that I once feared having regarding marital sex.

139

After all, I had quite a vault of memories from my sexual past. But from the start of our marriage, God gave me a relatively uncomplicated, really open, free, and good sex life with my wife. I have no other explanation for it except that God gave that to us as a gift. Now, to be completely honest, there were a few struggles in the very beginning. I did struggle with some difficulties related to the memories, causing me to have some other images in my mind when I was trying to be with my wife. I had to go through a period of confronting the issue and cleaning out those images so I could stay present. But, thankfully, it didn't take long for me to be able to work through that.

As a bit of an aside, my struggle with those images is not at all unlike the struggle many have with porn. It's the same type of process - where your sexual patterns and mental pathways are tied to the images that are stuck in your mind, rather than your present reality. Unless you go through a process of unlinking those images, your sexuality can be ruined for the rest of your life. Porn sets a trap to cause you to become completely self-focused. It causes you to merely respond to your memories, rather than acting in your present.

My marriage is an other-centered sexuality, as opposed to the self-centered sexuality that I spent years indulging with men. Prior to being saved, when I looked at another man's body – my first and strongest thought was comparison. "Damn, I wish I looked like that." It was envy. It wasn't attraction. Female beauty is very different. It's an "other-centered" attractiveness. It comes from a different place. To a man, female beauty is physical,

140

emotional, sexual, and spiritual all at once. My attraction to my wife comes from a completely different place in my soul. It's an attraction that compels me to marvel, to protect, and to meet her needs.

Married sex really defines your partner as a whole person, instead of simply seeing them as an object that's only there to offer you satisfaction. It's all just so very different. Sex with my wife is just very, very different. It's better. It's holy. It's just on a higher plane and a higher level than the self-centered, narcissistic, need-based sex that was all I knew as a gay man.

Chapter XXVI

I thought my time in school was done for awhile as we got settled into marriage and kids. But I kept having this thought that I needed to go to seminary. The one that kept coming to mind was in a southern state, which sort of felt like a foreign country to me. Plus, it was a Methodist seminary which, honestly, held no interest for me.

Gina came home from work one day and I was sitting with the baby in the living room. Now my wife is a very strong woman. She's not someone who lets others just walk over her. She can hold her own in any situation. When she acquiesces to something really quickly, I know it's God.

She walked in the door and was standing there, still holding her purse as she looked through the mail. And I just blurted out, "I think God is telling us that we need to move to Kentucky." This is a woman who has lived in Rome, Milan, and San Francisco. Demographically, let's just say she wasn't a good fit for Kentucky.

Gina looked up, was silent for just a moment, and nodded. "I think you're right. We should go."

So we did.

We both quit our jobs, packed up our apartment and our baby, and moved to Kentucky. We had no jobs and not much of a plan. I started grad school, and we ended up having two more babies during the three years that we were there. Honestly, we came to love living in a small town in the rural wilds of Kentucky. I think it was to warm us up to the idea of our eventual move to central Pennsylvania. After three wonderful years in small-town Kentucky, I graduated with a master's degree in theological studies.

Around the time I was nearly done with seminary, I was outside working in the garden at our house. By that time, my family dynamics back in Syracuse were changing as all of us were getting older. My uncle who'd been key to lots of family dynamics had died. Most of my cousins had move out of the area. My mother was divorced for a second time and living alone. And my Aunt Pat, who had always served as a warm memory for me, was now on her own. As I worked in the garden on that warm Kentucky evening, God was reminding me of Scriptures about taking care of widows and orphans. Then He said to me, "Your ministry is one person. I want you to go home and take care of the widow in your own family."

I brushed off my hands and walked into the kitchen where Gina was making dinner. As was our style, I came right out with it.

"I think God wants us to go back to Syracuse and take care of Aunt Pat and my mother."

In standard Gina fashion, she nodded as she looked at me for a few seconds. "I think that's it."

So, I turned down the job at the Georgia church and we packed up and moved up to Syracuse. After all of my schooling and student loans, I turned down a high-paying job to go take care of family. Not long after we got there, my Aunt Natalie was diagnosed with cancer.

Aunt Pat was ten years older than my mother. She and her husband, my Uncle Leo, were just in a different stage of life than my parents. Their kids were a lot older than my sister and me as well. When I was a young kid and my parents' marriage was unraveling, their kids were grown and out of the house. Aunt Pat and Uncle Leo would come get me quite a bit. Just me. They'd pick me up and take me to their house for the day, or sometimes we'd go to the movies. As a child, they were some of the few people who really meant something to me in the midst of the chaos. When she got sick, my cousins were not in a position to move home and take care of her. It just felt right for me to take care of her. It all goes back to remembering who you are more than declaring what you do.

As we were in the process of moving back to Syracuse, I accepted an invitation to attend a spiritual direction academy in Pittsburgh. It's a Catholic-based program that was affiliated with a major university there and was centered on the pioneering work of Fr. Adrian van Kaam. Fr. Adrian was elderly when I was there in the 1990's.

It's quite an intense academic program that's pretty hard to get into; at the time, this academy only admitted twelve people every two years. It's a bit less stringent now, but back then, if you applied and didn't get in, you had to wait two years for another chance. So when I got the invitation, I accepted it. The program required attendance at a week-long session on campus every four months. The rest of it was done remotely. I could make the drive from Syracuse to Pittsburgh in about five hours, so the proximity and the time seemed right for me to give the program my complete focus. God was really clear to me that this is what he wanted my time spent on.

By that point, it was becoming clearer to me that my destiny was more in the area of serving as a spiritual director rather than being a therapist or even a pastor. Earning the spiritual director credential from the academy was no mail-order degree. It's 36 post-graduate credit hours involving the study direction of anthropology, church history, and spiritual direction. I spent a lot of time reading Thomas Aquinas. It was an incredibly intense academic program, but with my return to Syracuse and with it happening at the same time I was serving my mother and my aunt, it all morphed into an important shaping time for me.

I understood the difference between spiritual direction and counseling. And I could see that, inherently, I was a spiritual director. (Catholics have this category in their framework, protestants do not.)

A spiritual director, counselor, and pastor all have overlapping job descriptions. I think it comes down to a matter of emphasis to draw the distinction between the roles. Let me give you an example.

Say a client with a sexual addiction comes seeking help from someone in each of those three roles.

- The pastor will listen and give biblical advice and scriptures to consider, and then point them in the right direction to get further help.

- The counselor/therapist will examine what's taking place in the addictive process in the client, and discuss things like behavioral triggers and what happens as a result of making poor choices.

- The spiritual director focuses more on always orienting the person toward God, no matter what moment he or she may be in, or what stage of the healing process.

As a spiritual director, I'm constantly looking for the roots of the behavior. I ask questions like how does what is happening affect your relationship with God? Where's the anxiety? Are you mad when this happens?

The goal of spiritual direction is for the person to have a transformative moment with Christ. I'm working primarily to open up the spiritual aspects of what's going on with them. That approach can be diametrically opposed to counseling psychology, which focuses more on equipping the person with tools to solve the problem.

In other words, spiritual directors start at the heart and work to push up through the spaghetti of the tangled thoughts that a client struggles with. A counselor or a psychologist or a therapist starts with the spaghetti and pushes down toward the heart issues.

So during this training to become a spiritual director, I thought back to the struggles I had as a photographer... how I would reduce everything about a person down to a single snapshot. While in this program, Father Adrian nailed me that I was doing this same sort of thing again. As I would assess a person, I would deal with them as a snapshot of their present, and effectively reduce them to a moment. I needed to look at the person in a total field of formation - the fact that they are coming from somewhere, they're going through something now, and they're heading toward a new circumstance. You simply have to look at a sum total of a person and all of their experiences, their hopes, their struggles. All of it. Snapping a shutter to capture a moment of time in a person's life reduces them to one flat, lifeless dimension.

During this course of study, something in me went four-dimensional. Every prism I used to look at the world, at people, at God... they all were radically changed. Growing up as a Catholic, I always had a nasty habit of looking at God as static. Like I'm here, and God's this thing over there. We each have our exclusive existences. Even at that point in my spiritual journey, I was prone to look at God as a father or an object. He was this thing that talked to me and ruled my life. That's just not how it is. He's not static at all. He's Himself within the trinity....within His own existence, He lives in a dynamic relationship between three persons...the Father, the Son, and the Holy Spirit. That fact alone proves why loving, healthy relationships between people — be it marriage, friendship, parent/child, or any other example — really reflects the essence of God.

The revelations I had and the changes I made at this time really started me on a course of looking at God differently, and correspondingly, looking at people differently. I think all that really re-shaped the course of my life and led to the most fundamental change in my life since I got saved.

I emerged from my time at the academy a completely different person. That all happened from 2003-2006, all when my kids were little. I still have strong relationships with many of the people I met while I was there. I go back for some of their one-week continuing programs... it feels good to go back and get some touch-ups and tune-ups every now and then.

After I finished the program, I felt like my life was sent into crisis. I had earned protestant pastoral credentials in seminary, but now with a more fully-orbed calling of spiritual direction, the Catholic church certainly seemed more like where I was heading. In order for me to be who I was supposed to be, I had to give up a pastoral career that I had been building for a decade. It was a difficult time as the road ahead for me clouded over significantly. But God helped me to realize that ministry is not a career. It's a calling. I had been busy building a secular version of a career with an overt focus on ministry, credentials, and degrees. He asked me to give it up. Actually, he asked me to destroy it. So during that time at the academy, I just didn't work for a couple of years.

When I was studying in this program, I really can't give you a good explanation about how our family made it financially, except for the fact that God just did it. I didn't work for three years and just went into a deep personal rebuilding time. Gina worked part-time, but other than that, I can't really define where the money came from - we just always had what we needed when we needed it. Gifts would just appear in the mail. Friends would knock on our door saying, "I felt like God told me to give you $400." Of course, that was a day when I needed exactly $400 to pay some bill. It was a really weird period of our life - but just as faith-building as it was weird. God really took care of us then in very tangible ways. We got through that time frame with three young kids and even had a fourth baby then.

It's humbling as a man to not be in the traditional "supporting-the-family" role, and even more humbling when it became clear God wanted me to turn down a job offer that I received to serve as an associate pastor with a mega-church just outside of Atlanta. My family would have had no financial concerns had I taken that job. I got the offer just before I graduated from seminary. I would be lying if I didn't say that it was enticing. But I knew the job appealed more to my ego than any sense of calling. My answer had to be "no."

Besides, God wasn't interested in my career. He was and is most interested in the best for me. A real man is a man who is not ego-driven but, instead, completely submitted to the will of God. He has always held me to that.

Chapter XXVII

I remember one fateful afternoon sitting in the driveway of that house in Syracuse. I truly had a moment with God when I was so pissed off at Him that, like Job, I was ready to curse Him and die. I sat in that car screaming and pounding on the steering wheel. God was making it abundantly clear that He did not want me to have a job. I'm not talking just a job in the ministry. He meant NO job. I couldn't find a job anywhere. I went to Wal-Mart and applied through their kiosk for whatever they had open. Seriously, even they wouldn't hire me. Here I was with a fancy theological degree and I was deemed unfit to even wear a blue apron while I greeted people and offered them a shopping cart.

Why wasn't I supposed to have a job? Because God wanted to support me and my family supernaturally. That's just the way it was. But my pride couldn't handle that kind of thing. My monstrously sized ego was beyond aggravated. Before I was really in a position to start serving people, God had to drive out my secret desire for ego-driven ministry. It's like He had to completely kill that part of me that cared so much about what others thought and had such lofty goals.

So, I sat there in that driveway, pounding that steering and cursing a blue streak. Then I stayed at nearly that level of being completely pissed off for at least another two weeks. Through that time frame, this rage was deepening. Soon it was all out in the open between God and me. I was supposed to BE somebody. I thought I was supposed to write a book and become a sought-after speaker and have a big-time ministry. My name was supposed to be one that was recognized as a legendary influence in the church community. Everyone loved to tell me how gifted I was - but I couldn't even get a job at a damn Wal-Mart.

About two weeks after my big blowup started in the driveway, this prophetic guy came up to me after church. (God seems to bring these kinds of people into my life at strategic times. I believe there are people who God uses to speak through when He wants a really specific message communicated. I'm grateful that He does this for me.)

"I feel like God has something He wants me to tell you," he said.

"WHAT?" Honestly, I almost snarled at the poor guy.

He took a hesitant step back. "Uh," he started quietly. "God says it's time to stop being mad now. It's gone on long enough. And you're in danger of going too far. It's time to put your anger away." Then he turned around and walked away.

I was stunned. This guy had absolutely no idea what was going on with me. This was a real moment of God "taking me to the mat." I was cursing God in my heart and sometimes even out loud. I was supposed to be somebody. And of all places, I was back in Syracuse ... SYRACUSE ... where I grew up and had vowed lots of times to never come back to. I had a house full of little kids and dirty diapers. DAMMIT, I had three degrees. I could have been working at a mega-church in Georgia. But my big task in life was to take care of a dying aunt.

I was mad that He was taking MY life away.

Now, I'm completely embarrassed about what I was thinking and how I was acting then. But God allowed me to go through it. He does that kind of thing. He was OK with me being that angry at Him and giving me an opportunity to let it out. Some people don't understand how God can take it when we're really pissed at Him.

But, if you let it go on too long, He'll let you know. After all, it's important to be respectful of your father. I let my kids get mad at me because it's human. But I'm not going to let them curse me out for two weeks.

God warned me through a prophet to cut the shit. And it worked. It snapped me out of it.

That was all about a year and a half into the time that we were back in Syracuse. It was around that time then that my Aunt Pat started to really decline. My mother, all of a sudden, began needing physical care as well.

Chapter XXVIII

It was probably about 20 years since my mother and I had what I'd consider a close relationship. We hadn't really spoken much since I had become a Christian, save for a crucial conversation that came about six months after I got saved. That was when I told my mother that I needed to cut off relating with her for awhile to get things on a better path in myself and in our relationship. She did not take that announcement well.

"I don't even know who the hell you are anymore. You're like a different person," she blurted out.

"Well, I am a different person."

I went on, "Mom, I think we're enmeshed and I think I just need some time to not talk to you and not come see you and not interact with you."

She was quiet when she asked me, "Do you think I'm the problem?"

Well, that was certainly no easy conversation.

"No, no, no, Mom. It's complicated."

I tried to make it clear to her how profound the change that my new relationship with Jesus was making in my life. How it was becoming obvious that I needed to closely examine some of the really unhealthy behaviors and relationships that were like rusted emotional anchors in my life, mooring me to behaviors I definitely needed to change. The torrential co-dependence I had had with my mother that had marked so many years of my childhood, coupled with the lingering rage of her abandonment, were still sunk deeply into my soul. I needed to get free of that tangling.

She wasn't happy, but she ended up giving me the space I needed to do the thinking and work needed regarding our relationship. In time, particularly after I got married, my mother and I started developing a pretty healthy relationship that had the appropriate boundaries and respect.

I moved away to go to college and grad school and was pretty intent on coming into my own.... And it was best for me to do that without having much influence from her. I talked to her maybe once a month. She visited when the kids were born, but there wasn't much else.

But while we were in New York to care for Aunt Pat, my mother unexpectedly had to retire from her job as a surgical nurse for health reasons. It soon became too much for her to maintain her house. But God had already put my family and me there. I was mowing both of their lawns. I was shoveling both of their driveways. I was busy not being anybody, while God had me there to serve. That season ended up being a real turnaround time for my mother and me.

So, after my dear Aunt Pat passed away and we left Syracuse in 2007, my mom moved with us to Pennsylvania. She lived with us until she died in 2015.

It was actually a great setup. She lived in our house, but in a separate little "mother-in-law" suite. She was back in my life again, and close, but it was boundaried this time. She wasn't co-dependent on us, but there was a closeness to us that was her own space. She had her own kitchen, bathroom, living room, and all that. But there was a literal door between us. My mother and my wife got along fabulously. She never criticized Gina and was always very respectful of her role as my wife. Mom was truly the textbook mother-in-law.

Mom was not constantly coming in to the house; she'd always knock first. She would always ask us before she gave the kids anything. During the eight years she was in our home, she was a real blessing. Gina and I would be exhausted with the kids and have little money to spare. However, we had the wonderful opportunity of being able to do little things like go for a walk together whenever we wanted because my mother was there. She was a built-in babysitter for years and really did a lot to make our lives easier.

I don't think she ever would have decided to live with us had we not gone to Syracuse to care for Aunt Pat. It really seemed like God's design for my mother to spend the last years of her life living with us. She got over all of her emotionally incestuous, clingy thing that she had with me and I started to know her as an adult. It's wise to remember that our parents are different at age 60 from what they were at 25. She was a different person and I was a different person. I think I can honestly say that she and I became friends through those last seven years.

I also helped her, I think. She was conflicted with what she believed about God. In retrospect, I can see that she took her time getting ready for her death, as she turned very reflective the last few years. It was obvious that she was really processing her life and her spirituality. We were able to share some significant moments with some conversations about God. Gina was a big influence on her too.

After being with us for a little over eight years, my mother got sick and died quite suddenly. There was only seven weeks between her diagnosis and her death.

When that diagnosis came, she got even more introspective and started processing on a very deep level. She delved deeply into the effects of growing up without her own father and some of the corresponding reasons of why she ended up marrying my father. The symbolic aspects of all of that was really weighing heavily on her. She was fighting to find meaning and closure in the few days she had left. Even though she wasn't a Christian, I think God was preparing her for death.

One morning, I went to her apartment and sat down just to chat with her before I left for work. It was apparent she was really low and she wasted no time in pouring out her heart to me.

"Honey, I feel like I was a terrible mother. I left you! I wasn't there for you all the way through. I should have stayed with your father a few more years to get you through high school."

Her list went on far beyond that. She was basically blaming herself for everything that had been wrong in my life.

I let her talk. And I sincerely meant it when I said it to her, "Mom, throughout everything in my early childhood, I always felt unconditionally loved by you. And that's the most important thing a mother can do for her child." I wanted her to know that, despite all that I went through in my teens and early 20's, she had invested a large measure of stability and strength in me that I was able to draw from during the tumult.

If I had any sense of being, any sense of personhood, any sense of value, it came from my mother's unconditional love. I knew I could screw up, do whatever in life and she would always be there for me. Now as an adult, I understand that she was, quite literally, not herself during that year that she abandoned me. That incident was the exception to the larger, more overarching nature of our relationship.

I continued, "Maybe you failed in some of the other stuff that mothers do or whatever, but you got the most important thing done. You communicated that sense of unconditional love to your child."

She looked away and was just kind of quiet. Then she looked back at me and nodded. That was a pivotal moment for the two of us. it was the last deep conversation that we had before she passed. But I could tell that something was

157

going on at a seminal level inside her, and I wanted to release her from any guilt that she was carrying.

It's funny, even though my father who was so closed down as a kid, he can talk about stuff from the past and childhood and all those things. He could find the words to explain things and get into stuff with me that my mother never could. Maybe that was her guilt. She felt differently about it than my father did. If I started to bring up stuff with her, generally she got defensive immediately and accused me of blaming her. She could never talk about things openly.

But, in that conversation shortly before she died, we did have that moment. I feel like it created a level of peace in her heart. I hope it did. it gave me a level of peace to be able to affirm her that, yeah we had our problems, but you weren't a complete shit mother. She was alright.

Overall, I think my mother felt loved by us. She picked up on that feeling of care and acceptance that we intentionally cultivate in our home. My mother's home, growing up, was chaotic and much of her early and mid-life was full of struggle. But at the end of her life, she lived in a home with calmness, stability, and a peaceful godly presence. I think it was living with us that gave her the environment she needed to relax enough to open up her heart and release a bunch of stuff from her childhood. God brought her to live with us because the introspection that it seemed like she needed wasn't something that would have been ignited just through a conversation or two. I feel like I had the opportunity to re-parent my mother as she worked some of this stuff out. That was a privilege.

If you've ever watched the television show, *the Golden Girls*, my mother was a Sophia. The blunt one with the acerbic wit. She was really funny. She graciously made my kids feel so special. Her last eight years ended up serving an important role in our family. They were really good last years with her. That was a gift.

My dad is ending on a high note too. It's amazing to see how God has brought lots of stuff for all of us full circle.

Chapter XXIX

"The only-begotten Son, of one substance with the Father, "God from God and Light from Light", entered into human history through the family"
- Pope John Paul II

The whole concept of "family" is terribly important; I see the function of healthy family as the arena where a soul can freely express what God brought it into the world to do and what God called it out to do. The family is key in nurturing an identity into full bloom. Family is, in and of itself, about the notion of incarnation... of creating life. And the fulfilling of family roles is terribly important.

Gina really sees the role of a woman as being a life-giver. She's right - women bring something to the table that men simply don't and can't bring. God has built a beautiful life-giving spirit...in the natural, the emotional, and the spiritual into women. I see men as being much more the provider and the protector. I think men have a key role in nurturing identity. Women may be the life-givers, but men are the ones who really call an identity out. A masculine nature shapes people in a different way than a motherly, feminine nature. But both are equally as necessary.

I think men discover the basics of manhood from other men, but women shape and call out aspects of masculinity that no man has the ability to do. That's why I so firmly believe that traditional gender roles are grounded in the anthropology of who we are. They're not just something that society has dictated. For us each to come into the fullness of our identity, we need that shaped and called out by the aspects of the truly feminine and the masculine. The fuel for that identity shaping comes via the roles in the family.

There is really something very holy about family. It's something very anthropological that God uses to shape us and to create us. But it can also distort us and destroy us if it's not healthy.

When I think about all of the distortion and loss of identity that marked my earlier years, I think it all happened because of breeches in my family. Had I grown up with a different type of family, I might have more solidly found who I was and who I was meant to be earlier, and not gone through everything that I did.

At some point shortly after I became a Christian, I really sought God for what my identity was to be. After so many years of distortion, I really had no idea what I was supposed to be at the core. I thought back to what God said to me on the morning that I was saved.

"You don't have to live like this anymore."

God wasn't fixated on my homosexual behavior. He was fixated on the deep despair of my soul. There was much more to restore in my life than simply not being gay anymore.

As a bit of an aside, I really hate the term "ex-gay." Actually ex-anything. May I encourage you to never define yourself by what your behavior was. If you've left something behind and embraced a new season, refer to yourself in the present. Never "ex" yourself from anything.

After Jesus changed everything in my life, I asked the Lord for what my identity really was to be - not ex-anything, but what it was to be in this new and changed existence that I was experiencing. God very clearly said to me, "My created plan for you and my providential will for you is to be a husband and a father. That's how I want to use you in the world. There's something I want to do that involves you being married and raising a family."

Many theologians say the purpose of marriage is not to meet your needs. It's to make you more holy. I think that's a lesson you're likely to learn that early on in marriage. Marriage, in the beginning....it's all woo-hoo! Lots of sex and that glow of being in love... marriage is great. Then you get into the work of actually figuring out how to live with each other. My wife's part Italian and part Jewish, so let's just say that the woman knows how to fight. About two years into our marriage, we had a doozy of a fight.

That night, everything went downhill fast. Once we got started, it didn't take long for me to hit the end of my coping skills with her. I was so mad. I remember thinking if I wasn't a Christian, this would be the night where she pushed my ego so far that I would leave and never come back. I was out on the couch and she was back in the bedroom. I was lying there talking to God about how absolutely pissed off I was at her. And the Holy Spirit really did something in my heart. I heard Gina walk out of the bedroom and down the hall, and suddenly my heart softened. I got up, grabbed her hand and started talking to her. And we got things worked out.

I tell that story as an example of the fact that, in a true Christian marriage, there are three of you in the relationship: the husband, the wife, and God. There's this buffer between the two human egos. It's not just two egos battering at each other and negotiating shared space. You run everything through that third partner - Christ - and you have a healthier, better relationship because of it. When honoring Christ as the higher perspective, on a different plane than just your two egos, it becomes easier to make your marriage more "other-centered", rather than a partnership that's simply focused on getting your needs met.

As I write this, Gina and I have been quietly chugging along in our marriage for more than 20 years. We're similar Myers Briggs-type personalities and really similar people in general. Over the years, the Lord has established a beautiful ease to our relationship. We both came from difficult families of origin. We both completely surrendered our lives to Christ. At the beginning, it was a foreboding thought to both of us to be married and have a family, as we were both secretly kind of thinking that it would be good if the family we created was different from the families we both had grown up in.

That's what we set out to do - and we've really enjoyed this process of creating a new family. We are both the first born-again Christians in our families. There are some who are devout in their religious beliefs, but we're the first real born-again Christians, at least among our parents and siblings. So we've prioritized creating a healthy, new culture.

Once we started having kids, they came every other year - boy, girl, boy, girl. As of this writing, they're 19, 17, 15, and 13.

This beautiful, overwhelming process of parenting - it's a gift. It's a gift to a guy who struggled so much with his identity when finding his own way as a kid. God told me there's something bigger in being the father in this family. I think of Abraham having Isaac and Ishmael as a promise of God, but he didn't really know what God was going to do to them. Who knows all the depths of God's purpose in reaching out to me and saving me, and then making me into a husband and a father. Maybe eight generations from now, one of my descendants will be a pope or a president or something. You really never know.

I do know that there is something spiritually relevant in my own life, and the lives of my wife and children, about me being a husband and a father. I have pursued it as a holy calling. From day one, I've had to totally trust

God for His enabling in those roles. I came into this with zero grid for being a parent. I had no idea how to be a father of any kind, let alone a good one. I relied heavily on the fathers who I knew. I spent a lot of time seeing how friends who were fathers did their jobs, and I talked to a lot of other men in church about how they went about it. Their insights were all helpful. But honestly, a lot of it has just been prayer.

There have been so many times, especially when they were little, that I had no idea what to do. So I prayed, "Lord, show me what to do." Show me what to do with this kid. Show me what she needs me to say to her right now. Show me what to do to help this kid not form a knot in his soul over this. Or whatever - I prayed that kind of prayer over and over again. And God gave me insight ... again and again.

Or sometimes the Holy Spirit would just nudge me to say something. There have been a few supernatural circumstances where I've turned to one of my kids and said something that totally shocked them. They asked, wide-eyed, "How did you know that?"

"God told me," I reply. And they get a little wigged out. And I smile.

My children are not perfect, but they are so much more grounded and healthier than I was as a kid. I'm extremely proud of my family. I truly think that being a husband and a father has been and is my life's work. It has nothing to do with my degrees or my job titles. It all has to do with my family being the core life work that God has assigned to me.

I have had lots of opportunities to make a choice to do something great with my career that would have led to me not being home as much or would have caused me to miss a bunch of my kids' stuff. And I always said "no" to those opportunities because I understood that my specific calling from God of being a decent husband and a decent father is the most relevant and central calling on my life.

There have also been times when one of the kids would come to me and I'd have a sudden flashback sear in my mind. "Oh you dumb son of a bitch!" I'd shut my eyes and picture my father in a rage. But then I'd hear it, I'd acknowledge it, and put my hand on my kid's shoulder and say, "Come on, I'll help you." Particularly when the kids were young, I was constantly wary of not repeating the mistakes my dad had made. It made me so happy to choose a different path.

As I write this, my father is terminally ill. Actually, a couple of years ago, he nearly died. One night that the doctors thought might be his last, he was talking to me on the phone.

He sort of whispered, "I see it, son. I see it." I had no idea what he was talking about.

"Your kids." He gasped for another breath. "You've changed it. You've changed the family. You did it. Your kids are so different. You did it."

He could barely breathe. He's slowly dying of emphysema. But even in his advanced age and regardless of the fact that he's still a pagan, my father can see what I did. He affirmed me for being a better father than he was. He actually said that, too, that night.

166

"You're such a different father than I was to you. You've done a great job. "

Boy, my earthly father really has blessed me in a lot of ways. As much as I felt cursed by him as a child, there have been significant moments in my adult life where God's really used him to bless me. The night he told me that, I definitely felt a validation of my life choices from the man who caused much of the damage that I had to heal from. A lot has changed from what life was like for both of us 40 or 50 years ago. He's a very different man now than who he was back in the 1970's.

With all that I've walked through in healing, and all that Gina and I have walked through in our marriage, I'm so grateful to have my wife and children be so central, so integral, in how my life's journey has unfolded. Honestly, when it all started, I really didn't want to do it. I really had to rely on God to show me the steps and to help me know what to do. I think Gina and I have succeeded. I guess time will tell. But our oldest son is off to college now and I just look at him and marvel. He is so radically different from what I was at that age. He's so much more together...sure of who he is. And far more kind and stable. All my kids have qualities that I just marvel at. I could write   a   whole   book   just   on   them.

Chapter XXX

There were certainly plenty of circumstances when I would have flashbacks to my father and would think about the steps I had to take to not repeat his mistakes. But it never crossed my mind that I would become my father. I just knew that wouldn't happen. God had simply done too much of a reversal in my life. I was to be the one to change the trajectory of generations in my family.

Honestly, one of my greatest joys is redirecting the family line. My children are so much more mature than when Gina and I were their ages. They're each so much more settled and developed in their true identifies. And they are happy. Their hearts are happy. My kids are not lost. None of them are lost in their lives or fear terribly what lies ahead for them. So, I think we've done something really well. Like every parent, we fear what we may not know about them, but we look at where they're each at and are thankful for who they've become and for where they're going.

My oldest son really started acting out one day, and quickly amped up into a full-on outburst. He was 18 at the time and really started getting snippy toward me, even throwing his weight around a little. Finally, as we launched into a fight, it came out. He needed something from me. It was a logical enough function that a father should think to do for his son, but it simply was not on my radar.

So I apologized and acknowledged it. "I'm really sorry. I understand what you're saying and I'm sorry that I have missed it up til now." I told him what he needed to hear from me and went on to explain.

"I'm so sorry. I was basically raised by wolves. By the time I was your age, I was out of high school and in my own apartment. When I was your age, going through what you're going through right now, neither of my parents were around. I didn't have parents for this situation that you're going through."

My mistake had been to put him in a place to do something on his own when the right thing would have been for me to help him. I honestly didn't know. It didn't occur to me that he wanted my help. That's the stuff that frightens me. I still have deficits and blind spots. It's not that I did anything intentionally or failed in any way as a parent to give my children something I knew they wanted. It's that I was completely oblivious of what was needed. Actually, I think that's true of every parent, as very few parents want to intentionally hurt their kids. But I just worry about... what the hell else did I miss? There are definitely times when I worry that any damage that I've

169

done to my children was because of my ignorance. But if that ends up being the case, I think they will be able to forgive me.

That's why single parents amaze me with all that they have to deal with. There have been so many times when one of our daughters has been struggling and Gina has just nudged me and said "just hug her." I'd raise an eyebrow at her. "Just hug her," she'd say again. "That's what she needs from you." Having that kind of input from the opposite gender is so crucial in parenting. I tell her the same sorts of things about our boys. "He's a boy. He's a teenager...that's what they do." She translates the girls for me and I translate the boys for her. As all the kids are either in or on the cusp of their teenage years, we're nudging each other more than ever with the things that they're all dealing with.

I don't feel like I personally had much to draw on from my past as far as parenting is concerned, but what little I have I've drawn from my Italian grandparents. I like to think that our home has some of the characteristics that I loved when I was at my grandparents' little white Cape Cod house. We work to make it full of love and a place where everyone who visits is welcomed. Plus, Gina loves to cook – she used to be a dietitian. She loves to experiment and play in the kitchen. It's actually one of the main things she does to relax. She cooks from scratch – you'll never be fed any processed food at our house. She's a first-generation American with a strong Italian heritage. Now that I think about it, I may have married my grandmother. A sexy blonde grandmother....

Gina and I work hard on "that feeling." When your kids are growing up "that feeling" in the home is paramount. My home growing up was permeated with feelings of rejection and shame. Gina grew up with a constant clench in her stomach because she knew her family was so unstable. Any day she could wake up and the family unit she knew was going to end. We both have this deep pall over our childhoods. So we devote ourselves to creating a feeling in our home that surrounds our kid with unconditional love and comfort. Of knowing that they're provided for, cared for, and protected. Every day, we want them to wake up that way and, every night, go to sleep with that same security.

I think that's a big reason why our kids are so stable. People comment to us all the time, "Your kids are so freaking together compared to other kids." My kids stand out. I rarely say it because I know it sounds arrogant. But my kids stand out at school... at church... really everywhere. As they mature, I think all four of our kids are beginning to realize that life and faith aren't about doing but about being. Gina and I work hard to create a stable home environment, send them in good directions, and let them make their own (hopefully wise) choices. I'm glad I had sons and daughters so I could get the full treatment and see them all start to come into their own.

I'm certainly not one who can or should be arrogant about being a parent. At the beginning, I was terrified. Like stone cold afraid that I was going to mess this up. But on the flip side, I was excited and really wanted to do it. I knew it was part of my destiny. I also knew that I couldn't do it on my own and that I'd need help....from my wife and from the Lord.

I remember one afternoon years ago when my kids were playing tee ball in the yard. We were living in New York and one of our neighbors had a dog who was part pit bull and was not well socialized. Any time you'd walk by that house, the dog would go nuts. That afternoon, that dog got out. My oldest kids were probably 7, 5, and 3. The baby was in the house. I was working in the garage and the kids were playing in the yard when that dog came flying across the street. Now, I'm terrified of dogs – honestly, I don't like them at all. But I didn't even think. The dog was hurtling across the yard, teeth bared and growling. I grabbed a baseball bat, jumped in front of the dog, and beat it off as it was hell-bent on attacking. The kids all got behind me, and then one by one, ran into the garage. They still remember the moment, because I was like a god to them as I fought off that dog. I will always remember that moment since fathers are designed to provide and protect. That was a landmark event for me when "protect" defined me in a circumstance when I might have been inclined to be fearful. I've learned that fathering overcomes fear when your kids are threatened. I would have strangled that dog with my bare hands if it would have kept my kids safe. That's just pure fathering instinct. That afternoon boosted my confidence as a father, because it helped me to discover some grit inside that I had no idea was there.

I can say with great confidence that fatherhood has made me a much better person. Marriage helps to steer me away from being self-centered. But having children does that in spades.

I know not everyone has kids or wants them. But for me, having children was essential for the deep healing that I needed from my narcissism. I go to work and bring home a paycheck, and 99 percent of my money goes toward providing for my family. Thirty years ago, I was a selfish little bastard. There was no one who I would have done that for. There's no one who I would have worked hard to support. But children make you "other-centered." And empathetic. And giving. And compassionate. And thoughtful. Being a father has made me into such a better person because I refuse to fail at being a father. For each of my kids, I've determined to be a really good father, so I have not hesitated to do what's necessary to achieve that. It's almost been like a discipline for me. I think that's why God said to me, "It's My plan for you to be a husband and a father." He knew how essential it would be in my life. Because I can see the maturity that its brought about in my life. I needed it. Other people can take other paths to that kind of growth and maturity, but being a parent... I needed it.

I can never disappoint my kids emotionally. When they look at me and and I know they need something from me (not an iPad but a true need) I drop everything for them. They know they matter. I've been very cautious about those unspoken messages with my children. That's part of creating that nurturing atmosphere, that "feeling" in the home. My wife and I work for that every day. It doesn't happen on its own.

Gina's home life as a child was pervaded by dread and anxiety. Her parents were always at odds and nothing ever got resolved. She watched those relationships devolve year after year. And it had a huge impact on her.

She's been really big on not going to bed mad, and that's a big reason why we almost never fight. She's also wisely cautious. If our kids see us have an argument, she makes sure they see us apologize to each other and resolve it. We did have one really big fight – I knew it was getting really bad when she started swearing at me in Italian. I think I've only made her that mad maybe three times in our 20 years of marriage. But we got things worked out. Later that evening, we were all at dinner laughing and joking, and my son asked cautiously, "Is everything OK here?" I just explained to him, "Your mother and I are both passionate Italian people. That means we love each other deeply and we fight really hard. But then we're over it just as quickly because the bottom line is that we really love each other."

I always try to frame that for the kids that if they hear us snapping at each other, it's temporary and we'll get through it. Gina and I both endured that kind of thing every day growing up and we know how that kind of fear can be so corrosive.

My kids know that their parents love each other. That's the foundation for any feeling we create that's good in our home. Can I just encourage you....don't get married if you're not going to get along with that person. Forget about money, or houses, or social stature and all that other stuff. Just marry someone you can get along with. Why

174

would you want to live for decades with someone you
don't like?

Chapter XXXI

Have you ever been at the right place at what feels like the wrong time? Honestly, that kind of thing happens to me all the time. The Lord directs me into a place where the initial reason I'm there doesn't work out, but it ends up being the right place as His plan continues to take shape. That's what happened to me when my family and I moved to Pennsylvania.

A position opened up at a fairly big church there and it felt like the directive from the Lord for me not to work had shifted. We prayed and considered, and decided to make the move. The job came with a good, family-sustaining salary. It was a titled role, and it even came with a nice office with a big window. Everything about it felt like what I should be shooting for. But as soon as I got started at the church, I knew it was wrong. It was another choice that I made based on ego. And that hunch didn't take long to be confirmed...the church restructured not long after I started and my position was eliminated.

The church leaders told me on a Sunday that my job was ending. I went home and told Gina, while trying to fend off pretty panicky feelings. On Monday morning, I heard the rumbling of a motorcycle in my driveway. I looked out the window to see this prophetic guy that I had met a few times. He rides a motorcycle and he hears from God. Not a bad gig if you ask me. Anyway, he showed up at my house and told me he felt like God had told him there was someone who he was supposed to introduce me to. That person turned out to be the director of a counseling ministry in Pennsylvania.

This guy was actually in the process of trying to leave the director's job, as he really just wasn't happy in the role. Even though I said that I'd never lead a counseling ministry, I thought the setup with this prophetic guy at least warranted my time in meeting him. We started meeting for coffee pretty regularly to talk about the ministry and who might be a better fit for the position. He ended up pushing past my reluctance and convincing me to apply. He told the ministry's board about me and after a few meetings, they officially offered me the job. I've been there ever since.

After my time as a pastor, taking a job leading a counseling ministry was something I honestly did with some reluctance. But it did feel like the right time and the right place. Honestly, I'm still a reluctant director. I love working behind the scenes...that's why I have no interest in being the "face" of the ministry. I like to coach. I like to fortify the counselors to constantly grow in their service and insight. I like to be the spiritual director and constantly be the one who's looking for the spiritual roots and how the Lord is moving in any situation.

Part of the appeal in me taking the job was that I knew I would have a chance to really shape the place. The board courageously gave me full latitude to help chart the course of how the ministry would grow and serve. From my start there, they understood who I was and what I wanted to do. I came in with a multi-year plan and they completely supported me in every step of implementation. From my background, they knew I intimately understood the struggles that many of their clients face. It turns out that I've ended up being a perfect fit for leading this type of ministry. As always, God absolutely knows what He's doing.

It's been my privilege to create a tiny portrayal of the church at this ministry. We work together each day to try and do things in the way that really addresses core needs in broken people. People who are struggling with same-sex attraction, or bound up in pornography addiction, or fearing that their marriage is over need tender care. I wake up every day motivated to keep shaping our team of counselors to lovingly care for these people who have come to us. They've reached out because they have at least a glimmer of hope that God can change their lives. Because I'm a living, breathing example of His work, I wake up every morning determined to create an environment and a team that will serve as God leads in helping these dear people find healing and peace.

Chapter XXXII

It's complicated when you're a victim of sexual abuse. For the sake of expediency, the world likes to paint it as something a little more simple. But, trust me, it's a more complex journey when it's happened to you.

In the first few years after I got saved, I could be very cavalier about my abuse story because I had severed my emotional connection to it. It took me a good decade before I could really engage and understand the horror of it. It takes a long time for that to come out.

When I was a terribly screwed up 12-year-old boy, my perception of what happened is that I went after this guy who was meaningful in my life and I seduced him. It was all my doing.

But that wasn't real. What was real is that I was 12 and he was 21...and it all lasted until he was 23.

I did know it was horrendous though. But that was just one part of the boiling stew that is childhood sexual abuse. The knowledge that the behavior is wrong is at the heart of what many abuse victims experience. They often have a religious upbringing and know enough to define it as aberrant behavior. But the knowledge that it's wrong isn't convincing enough to deal with the compulsive need they may have to engage in the behavior.

Or perhaps the scenario is that God is not present to them in a real tangible way, but this behavior is. I know I felt that. I had prayed my whole childhood for my family to get better. And the thing I was asking God for never happened as a child. So being an active participant in this horrendous scenario was a tangible part of my rejecting God. Or the interpretation was sometimes that God hadn't answered me — so, He wasn't there. But this man was. And in that moment, that was more important.

No matter the breadth of components in the morass of feelings that sexual abuse causes, every victim deals with all sorts of guilt. My situation certainly engendered all sorts of guilt in me. I first started expressing it by complaining about the church and how stupid everything about it was. I was justifying my rejection of the church and all things related to God so I could justify doing whatever I wanted.

But that wasn't real. What was real is that I felt tremendous guilt and shame. Those weren't new feelings for me with everything I faced in my childhood. I was already swimming in that soup. The abuse just caused another round. It was deeper this time, though. Much deeper.

I lived with this constant scream inside of me. This tension and this horrible feeling of being empty inside from the rejection of my father. While I was in another man's arms being "loved", that feeling was stilled for awhile. It started with my abuser. And I sought it in the arms of more than a thousand other men. That feeling was so powerful. And is for those who are still trapped in its lie. It's like an opioid.

Sex unites you at this deep level. Here's what I've learned: if you got damaged at your core, a sexual addiction is going to happen because it's the only thing other than God that is strong enough to still the hurricane of shame. The problem is that sexual addiction is external so you have to keep getting more and you have to keep compromising yourself. With another person, you're getting momentary relief but you're surrendering your power to another person. It does do something for you. It's just that you pay a price.

The only thing that can truly address and reverse that addiction is God. The very presence of God is the companion needed to overcome the stifling loneliness that shame commands. The beautiful affection of God fills all the deficits. And the life-changing power of God helps you to learn to be in control of your body's behavior. For a victim of abuse, He really is the only one Who can truly bring about change and healing.

Chapter XXXIII

I've always had a special affinity for pin oak trees. Through the winter, you can often see one with its brown leaves still clinging to the branches even through a biting February wind. A pin oak will hold onto its dead, bleached-brown leaves all winter long, and only shed them once the growth in a new season begins. Honestly, I think the pin oak is a beautiful symbolism of what a work in progress looks like.

Every time I see one, God reminds me that I was like a pin oak. You can't just expect the leaves to all disappear and then, magically, see beautiful new growth appear one day. Change, especially a change from a homosexual, broken lifestyle, is a process. It's organic. It involves the human heart. It's not a step-by-step program or a series of boxes that you just check off as you go. A healing journey is different for everyone who goes on one. Different paces, different times, different routes. Some people have to be wooed a little more than others. Some people are ready to go.

Healing and change isn't something you can really quantify in a book or a course or an outline. My own journey of change isn't something I could ever just transpose on to something else. It's incarnational to walk with other people who are on that type of journey. You have to be prepared to just walk with them and let them find themselves at their own pace. It's disrespectful and, indeed, harmful to push them farther and faster than they can go at any given time. The new growth will be what pushes the old, decrepit leaves off of their branches. That growth will come at a different pace and from a different depth for every person.

The healing needed in my own story had to come from about as deep as it could get. The breach I had with my father was very fundamental in my personhood. I can think way back to a night when I was still in diapers...I'm going to guess I was maybe about two and half years old. For some reason, my father was alone at home and had to watch me. This was in the late 1960's when no man - let alone my hyper-masculine father - was expected to watch his own kids.

I don't know where my mother was, but my father had to change my diaper and he couldn't do it. I'm terribly young, small, lying on my back on a bed, and my father is looming over me, swearing and fussing with my cloth diaper. I actually tried to help him. I remember pointing and saying, "Mommy puts the pin here."

"GODDAMMIT, shut up! I know what I'm doing."

That's the first memory I have of my father. Actually, it's my first memory ever. I say that to relate how very deep this warped identity is in my persona. I made choices to close myself off to him almost as soon as I had the capacity to do so. I built an emotional wall between us because I wanted some form of protection. Then by extension, I built a wall between the real me and all men. And then because I am a man, I built the final wall between anything male that was inherent in my nature.

This stuff goes really, really deep in people. Only God can fundamentally bring change to that depth of a rift. But I can't stress enough to all of you who are relating with those struggling on this type of journey - you can't just rip this type of brokenness out of people. You can't just "call" it out of them and expect them to respond positively. You definitely have to be prayerful, cautious, patient, and long-suffering in most of cases with them to provide an environment where the new growth starts to sprout and the old leaves start to fall off.

Let's just commit to giving our brothers and sisters, these beautiful works-in-progress, the time and support they need to summon the growth, forgiveness, and newness that pushes off the decrepit leaves that might still be clinging long after some might expect the dead season's symbols to be gone. Change... powerful, life-giving change...   takes   time.

Chapter XXXIV

All through my childhood, I was misshapen by my father. My identity was completely distorted. I've talked before about how most of my childhood was spent cowering from my father, when he was constantly belittling me, or smacking the side of my head, or towering over me yelling and spitting. It really was god awful. With some distance now, I can track the two big psychological effects of that on me.

My reaction to my father totally came out in really strong passive-aggressive behavior toward men. My father's actions generated such a rage in me that I really generalized my hatred for him onto all men. I hated all men because they were like my father. Masculinity, to me, meant being aggressive, controlling, and hateful. But at the same time, because I constantly craved affection from my father, I also transferred that craving to all men. Though I hated them, I craved their attention, love, and affection. Oh my, what an unbalanced psyche I had.

All of that unbalance totally expressed itself in my sexuality. My weird, split life was a significant part of why I was such a crazy-maker with the men I was involved with more than casually. I had this volcanic need for love and acceptance and for them to affirm me. But at the very same time, I hated them. I flat out wanted to hurt them. I wanted to get back at my father by hurting every man I came in contact with.

I was really drawn more to straight-acting men much more than the really effeminate gays. There was a part of me that enjoyed pulling them into homosexual behavior because it felt like I was degrading them and tearing them down. I was hurting them by harming their masculinity. By feeling like I was stripping them of their manhood with gay sex, I felt like I was enacting revenge on my father through these other men and working out that rage and anger that I had toward him.

But, at the same time, I would submissively do anything they wanted. In every relationship with a man, I would vacillate between that hurtful aggressiveness and this "I need you, don't be mean to me" by being very vulnerable and needy with them.

I only had one model to draw from as I lived in this ten year "raging period" of my adolescence and young adulthood: that warped relationship with my father that caused hatred and a desperate need for love from men. It was that split psyche that totally set me on the wrong path to seeking what I thought was love from other men.

I really like plants and gardening. The rhythm and seasons of their color and life. The creativity that they bring out in me. The pulling out of the unwanted weeds and the tender stoking of growth. God really uses nature and gardening metaphors with me all the time. I have a huge organic garden. I don't use fertilizers or pesticides. Never have. I do everything with composting and all natural stuff.

We bought a house that, with a few minor exceptions, had a yard formed of just a half-acre triangle of grass. Over the years, I've landscaped it and terraced it into this really beautiful park-like piece of land. It's a creative thing that I do with God. The gardening metaphors where He shows me things and the ways that He speaks to me as we till and create together have been very shaping for me.

I was a pretty sensitive kid. I had a softness. I loved plants and gardening even then. But man that plant sensitivity was something that really drove my father nuts. He hated that his son would be that soft. That empathetic and nurturing. It soon became obvious that part of his cruelty toward me was his effort to "toughen me up" and get that out of me.

My mother had a lot of houseplants around the house and I loved being their caretakers. If one of the plants was failing, I used to take it to my room to give it some extra care. Or I'd break off a piece and root it, or pot it in my room and bring it back to life. I liked nurturing the sicker ones.

One day, my father came in my bedroom and saw this plant on the corner of my dresser and he completely flipped out on me. It was just a little plant...one that my mother had almost killed. I had taken a tiny little snippet off of it and nursed it back to life. It was doing really well, and I would soon have brought it back down to the dining room where my mother kept her plants.

"What the FUCK do you have this plant in your room for?" My father was enraged.

"Boys don't have plants in their rooms. That's a sissy thing."

And he grabbed the little shoot of a plant in the pot.

"NO! Leave it alone! I like it," I screamed.

I watched helplessly as he flipped it upside down and hurled it in the garbage can. The tender, young plant was destroyed. I had hovered over it, nurturing it to grow. And my father destroyed it in a rage simply because he was embarrassed by a son who would be so soft. It was really traumatic for me.

My father's behavior cursed my identity. He didn't just not bring it out. He cursed it. Totally misshaped it and cursed it.

In that healing process where I spent four months alone in my apartment, Jesus brought that up to me. "You know, your father cursed a part of your identity that I gave you as a holy thing."

A different father would have recognized that empathy and called it out of me and shaped it for good. But God as my Father called it out and was able to redeem and re-shape after I accepted Him into my life and was listening to Him.

I am an empathetic person... sometimes too much. I still like to nurture things. I would rather buy a sapling than a fully grown tree and have the joy of watching it grow and change over the course of a decade. I don't want to be in a landscape that's done. I like the dynamic of filling it in and nurturing it to beauty. Even through painful but necessary pruning.

Perhaps that joy in nurturing growth is what's given me a great appreciation for process. The growing. The nurturing. The pruning. The blooming. I think it's also had a direct correlation in me becoming a spiritual director and leading a program for people with sexual addictions, post-traumatic behavior and stress from sexual trauma. It's a process. There's no magic bullet that heals people overnight. There's always this long process that requires lots of steps in eventually achieving a thing of beauty. I like that. I like that process of hovering over them. And pruning here and misting there. Even adding a little composting when needed. Being a part of helping people to heal and change is like a garden to me. That's how I see people. It's a gift to be able to watch God nurture and grow the good things that are taking seed in their hearts, while not letting the weeds choke out the good.

Chapter XXXV

My encouragement for anyone helping someone with "issues" like mine is this: *stop obsessing on the behavior.* Be less concerned about people's sexual orientation (and how they act it out), and be more concerned about their spiritual orientation. Who they're having sex with and why they have those desires is a symptom of what is rarely addressed: *the gnarled root of pain that they've likely been carrying in their hearts since they were small children.*

A guy might get saved and still be having sex with men 20 years from now, but in his heart he's striving after Jesus. I'm a story with a clear turning point who ended up with a great wife and a family. Believe me, that does not happen to everyone who has stories that start like mine. Some people choose to be single the rest of their lives. And there are some people who haven't yet had enough re-ordered in their inner life to be able to stop the compulsive behavior.

Honestly, I think that's all OK to God. That's where I get in trouble because it seems like I'm being soft on sin. But I really don't think that's the case. It's how people function with these disorders. In my opinion, it's best to recognize the reality of the present, and couple it with instilling a hope in the person that change really can come as they keep walking the path.

You simply cannot lay a grid of expectations on anyone. Every individual has to walk on their own path and work at their own pace ....you just can't push the pace of grace. You have to let people find their way in the wilderness - and like the Israelites in the Old Testament, it might take 40 years to get anywhere better.

It hurts me when I see clients at our ministry or other people who I relate with getting the type of treatment from the church that makes them have to work so much harder for their healing. When they're creaking open the door to asking Jesus to help pull out the deep root that they've lived with for decades, you don't just hand them a book and lecture them on their behaviors. Dealing with people with this type of fragile, broken spirit requires a very individualized approach. You can't "snapshot" people. You have to look at every single person and let him or her own an individualized story, and permit them to be different from every other person. Some may be walking similar types of paths, but every person brings their own history, their own pain, and their own places that need a loving, transformative touch from God.

I understand that many people will need help far beyond what the local church is equipped to give. That's why ministries like the one that I serve with exist. But these people need faith-filled companions to be with them on the journey toward healing. And I believe they should legitimately hope to find these types of companions in the church.

So, here's my most sincere advice if you desire to serve as that type of compassionate and helpful companion for someone on their journey. See the person. See the individual. Don't generalize. Don't see the person as part of a large category where everyone can be painted with a broad brush. Be calm. Be kind. Be forgiving. There will be days when they regress. The path forward is not a straight line. Don't worry about loving too much.

Working with a caring and competent ministry and walking with compassionate companions provides the atmosphere for God to change lives. I've seen Him do it. I'm a living testament to Him doing it. I want to see so many others have that same opportunity.

Chapter XXXVI

I would offer that pride is the primary problem with all of humanity. Pure and simple pride. An overt preoccupation with one's self. Or perhaps at more of the heart of the matter, pride says that what I believe, that what I think, even what I define myself as, cannot be questioned. It's no coincidence that the gay movement blankets all of their actions and agenda with the term pride.

It's a dangerous place to be to declare that no other viewpoint is as valid as your own. Or that nothing else can provide definition to your life aside from what you say can. That's what happened with me. I deemed what defined me - my abuse, my horrible relationship with my father, my need for intimacy, my "fabulous" gay trappings, my hopelessness, my narcissism. I was unwilling to surrender to anything outside of myself.

Until I completely crumbled emotionally. And God told me "You don't have to live this way anymore." I no longer had to live in a way that I had to carry the weight of being the definer of all things about my life. What an incredible relief.

I was no longer trapped in an identity that was defined by brokenness and pride. I was now, rightly, defined as what I was created to be. A person who was created in the image of God, the very One who created all things.

> *For in him all things were created: things in heaven and on earth, visible and invisible, whether thrones or powers or rulers or authorities; all things have been created through Him and for Him. - Colossians 1:16*

Understanding the accurate nature of our creation is so crucial, especially in light of how so much of what's going on in our culture is focused on self-identifying. Self-identifying a gender. Self-identifying "truth." Self-identifying a destiny that is minuscule and lifeless compared to the destiny that God has designed. It's all so pagan. It's all so wracked with destructive pride.

I can say unequivocally that pride, and all of the relational disorders that it causes, can only be dealt with by surrender. A surrender of everything deep inside you. But it's not a once-and-done deal. It's a daily surrender. It's a chipping away at the problems that pride causes. Surrender isn't easy. Surrender isn't pleasant. But it's a far better option than living a life where you're nothing but lost in yourself.

> *"So God created mankind in his own image, in the image of God he created them; male and female he created them." - Genesis 1:27*

We are created beings. We have a Creator who, amazingly enough, bestows esteem and value on us by creating us in his very own image. We are given definition by something outside of ourselves. We each have a unique perspective and a personal set of circumstances, but we were created to be identified through bearing the image of and recognizing our relationship with our Creator.

Scripture is full of examples of what happens when the human mind gets too full of itself, and is swayed by lies, and simply gets lost. And we're seeing those same things happen today with the incredible gender dysphoria and confusion to which so many people fall prey. I don't doubt the sincerity of people when they say they believe they're something that they're not. They really do believe it. But their belief is simply their own opinion - it's not founded in anything beyond their own mind and their own pride.

The only way to escape that trap is to see who you are in comparison to a constant. We all have to have a true North to have any idea about any other direction. I now know beyond the shadow of a doubt that we have to have a Christian framework to see where something has gone wrong. God is our Creator and all things have been created through Him and for Him. The only chance we have of seeing things as they really are is to view them in comparison to the framework He's established. To view the lies we've believed in light of His truth.

But God offers more than a framework. He offers us so much more than what we identify ourselves as. He offers us true and actual identity.

"Yet to all who did receive him, to those who believed in his name, he gave the right to become children of God." - John 1:12

"See what great love the Father has lavished on us, that we should be called children of God! And that is what we are!" - 1 John 3:1a

Your true and actual identity - who you really are - is a child of God. A powerful, glorious, valued, beautiful and non-negotiable identity.

But whether or not you surrender to who you really are is up to you.

Acknowledgements

My thanks to my co-writer Diane Moore, without whom this book would never have been written. Her patience, expertise, and artistry is what enabled my story to make its way onto the printed page.

DianeMooreMedia.com

Made in the USA
Middletown, DE
25 June 2018